CITIES SKYLINES

A COLORING BOOK FOR ADULTS GENERATED BY A.I.

Table Of Contents

In Collaboration with AI

The images in this book were created from collaboration of the author and sophisticated artificial intelligence (AI) software. The images were derived from detailed and specific instructions on different theme based software programs. Following this instruction, AI then generated the detailed and unique images in this book. A viewpoint like no other, these images won't be found anywhere but within this book. We hope you enjoy hours of entertainment creating masterful coloring pieces.

Let The Gray Guide You: A Quick Start To Gray-Scale Coloring

Gray-scale coloring books offer a great way for beginners and talented artists alike to enjoy the art of coloring. Gray-scale images are created using various shades of gray, which makes it easier to create stunning results without worrying about color blending or shading. When it comes to coloring in gray-scale, there are many techniques that can be used. First off, you want to make sure you have the right materials, such as pencils, markers or watercolors, that will work with your image. We suggest a good set of colored pencils for the intricate details you'll find in this coloring book. It is also helpful if you use a light source, so that all the different tones can be seen more clearly when selecting colors. Once these supplies are gathered together, then it's time to get started!

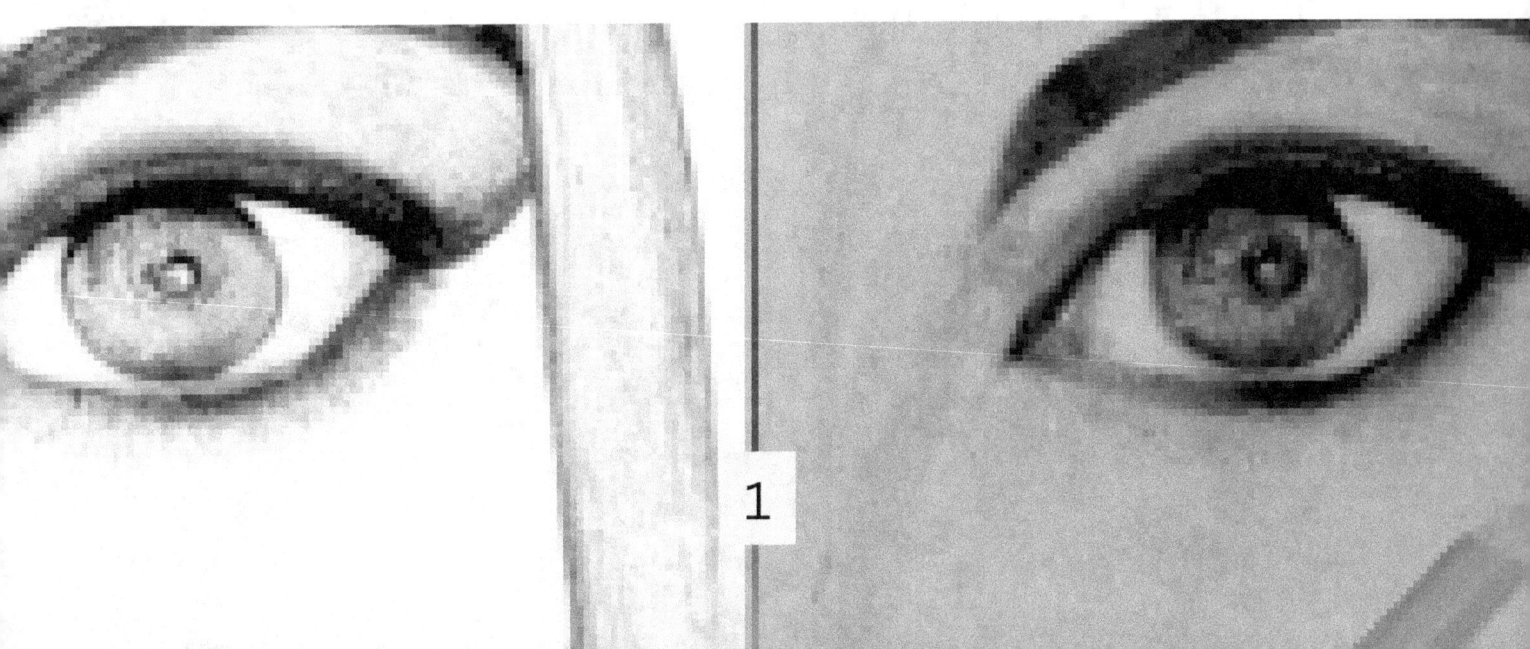

1

There are many techniques you can learn with experience coloring gray-scale, and we are going to touch on a few before you get started. However, the main idea and a good rule of thumb is to let the gray guide you with your coloring. For light shading grays use light colors and for dark shades of gray use darker colors. A little like coloring by numbers, except you are letting the different shades of gray be your numbers. Going from light to dark choose sets of colors that would fit well in the grays color spectrum. As more pressure is applied, the gray gains intensity and becomes darker gradually. Choosing a color for each phase or level of gray intensity will set you up great to have a stunning final result. Using this overall main method will have you producing amazing colorings before you know it.

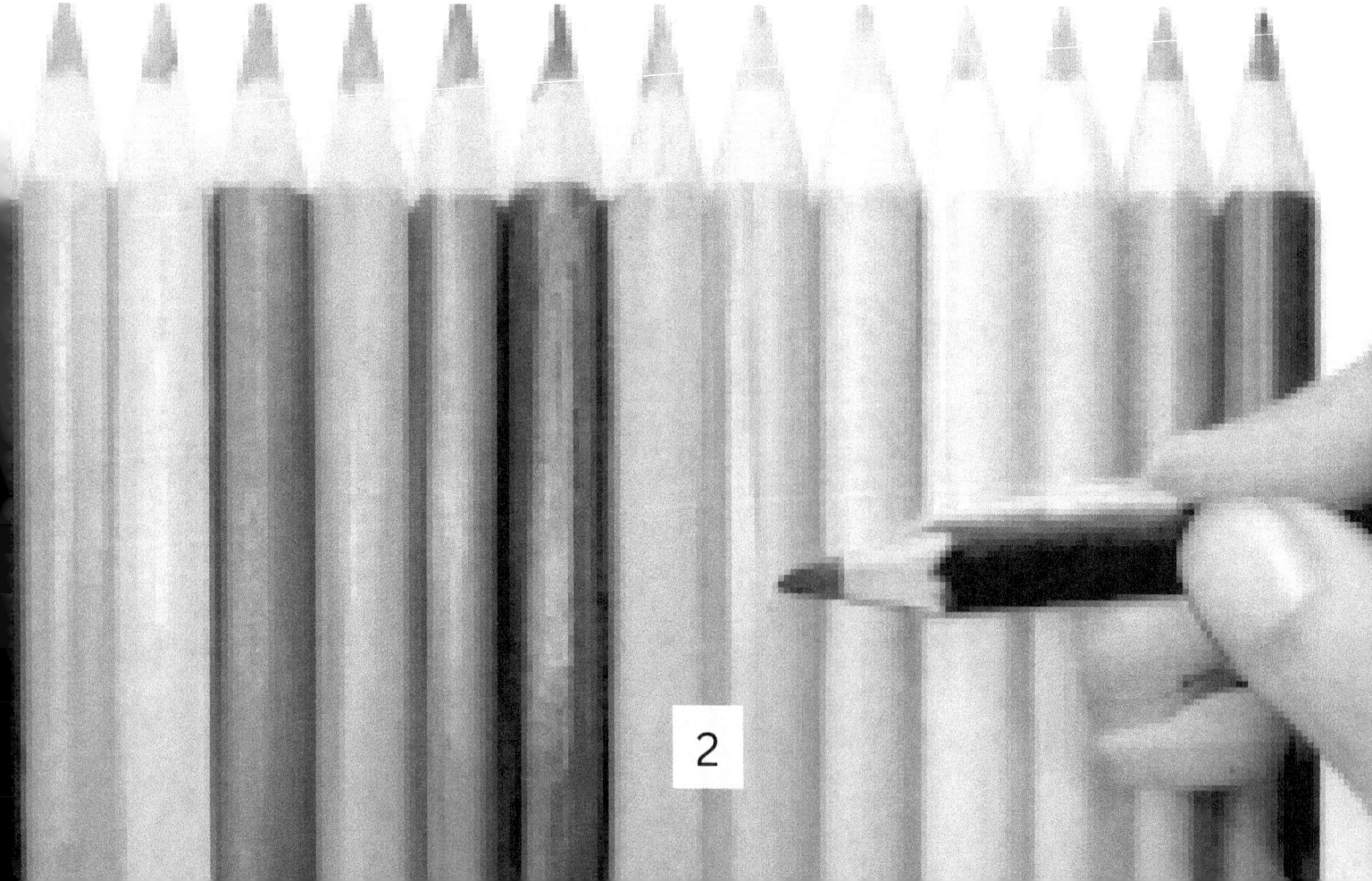

As experience comes, there are many developed techniques to learn. One technique for coloring in gray scale is called "Blocking," which involves applying one solid block of color at a time within an area on the page, instead of gradually building up layers of shading and hues as one would do with traditional full color images. This technique works best when working with larger areas like backgrounds or clothing items, where detail isn't necessary, but rather we need just overall coverage for a pleasing effect. Another approach could involve adding texture by using crosshatching lines throughout certain areas, before applying color on top. This gives an interesting look, while still keeping things looking simple and clean. Lastly, adding highlights and shadows through layering darker and lighter shades within each area allows depth while still staying true to its monochromatic style. This is done by creating gradients between two different tones (such as black & white), rather than multiple colors like what would be done with colored pencils/paintings, etc...

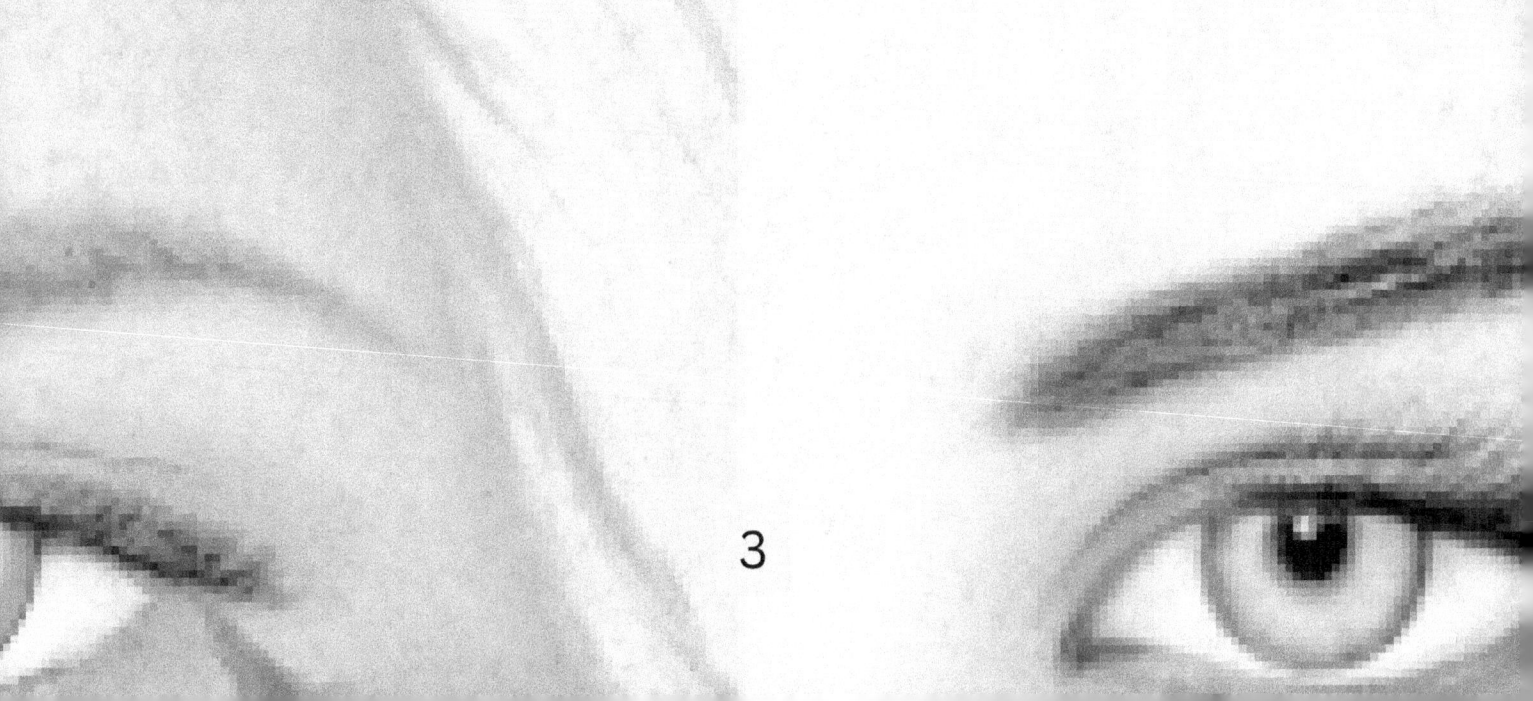

By utilizing these tips, along with varying amounts of pressure applied during application—from light strokes that barely show up on paper all the way down heavy saturation —one can easily take any single gray scale image from dull & lifeless into something vibrant & beautiful! Beginners may find they prefer blocking their design first, before moving onto more intricate detailing. On the other hand, experienced colorers might dive straight into mixing & matching textures/shades until they achieve their desired outcome. Artificial Intelligence (A.I.) generated all the images in this book, which provides a unique approach to Gray-Scale coloring and some truly eye-catching artwork once finished! The images below the text are great to practice the different techniques you can use, and showcase the stunning results that can be achieved with gray-scale coloring. We hope they serve as inspiration as you color your way through the stunning skylines in this book.

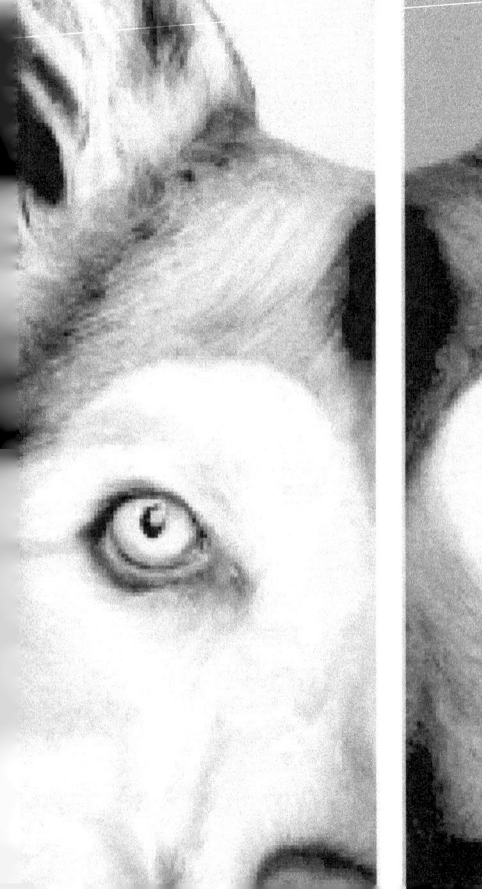
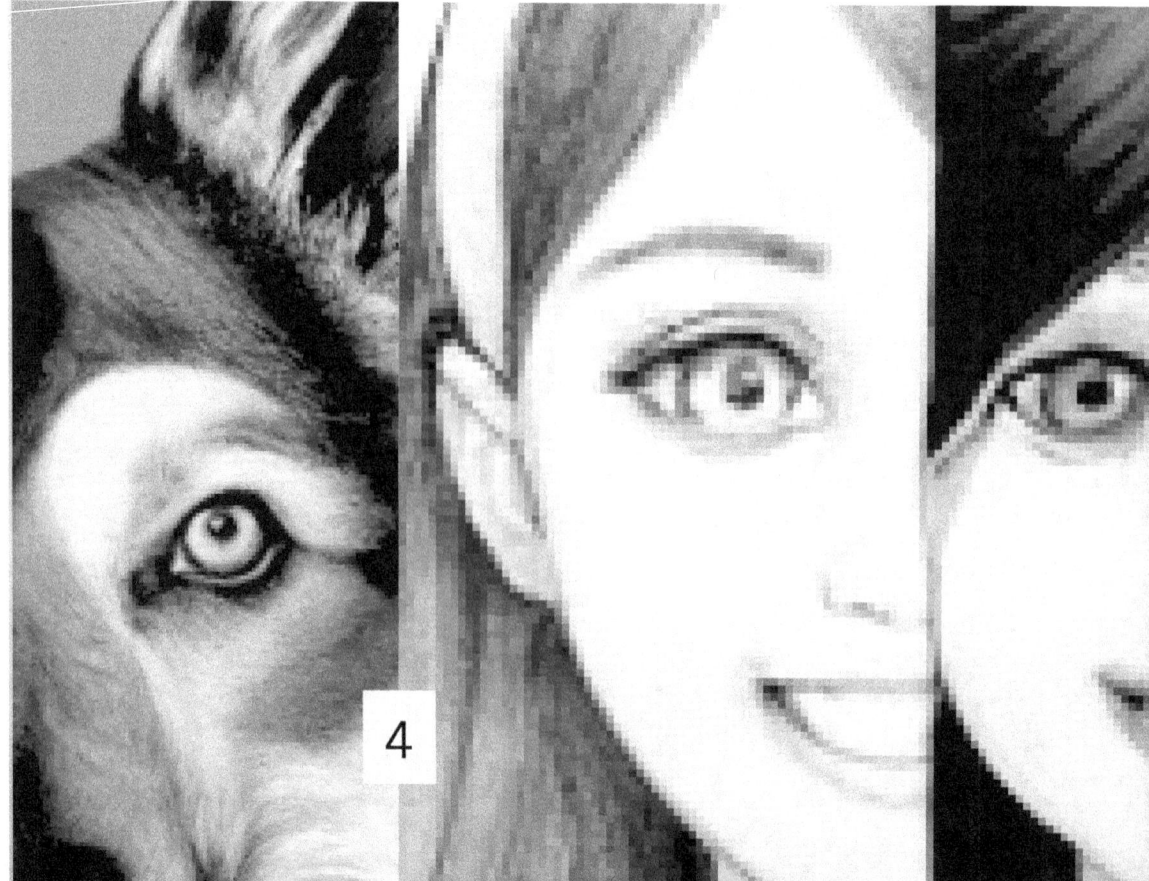

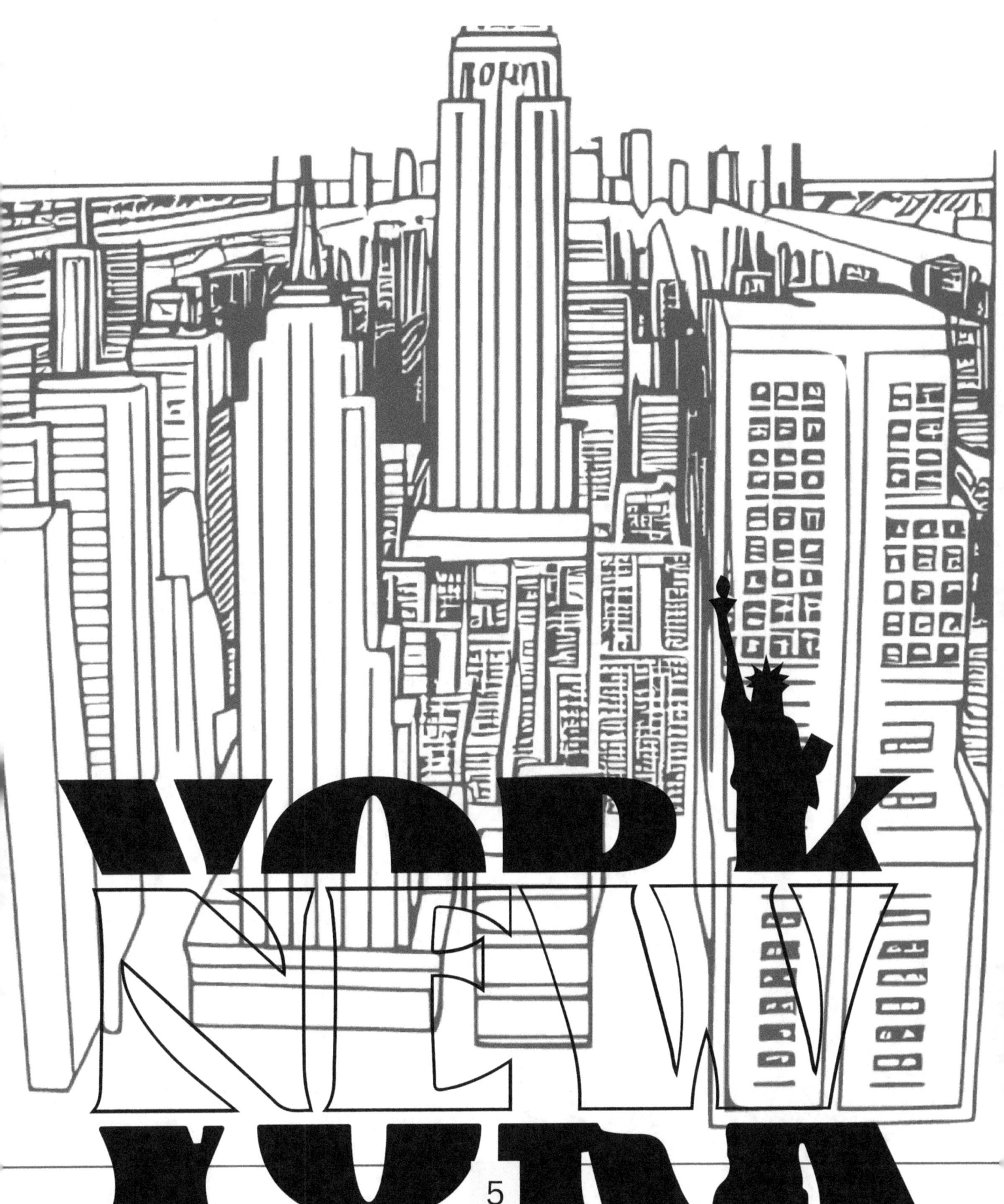

5

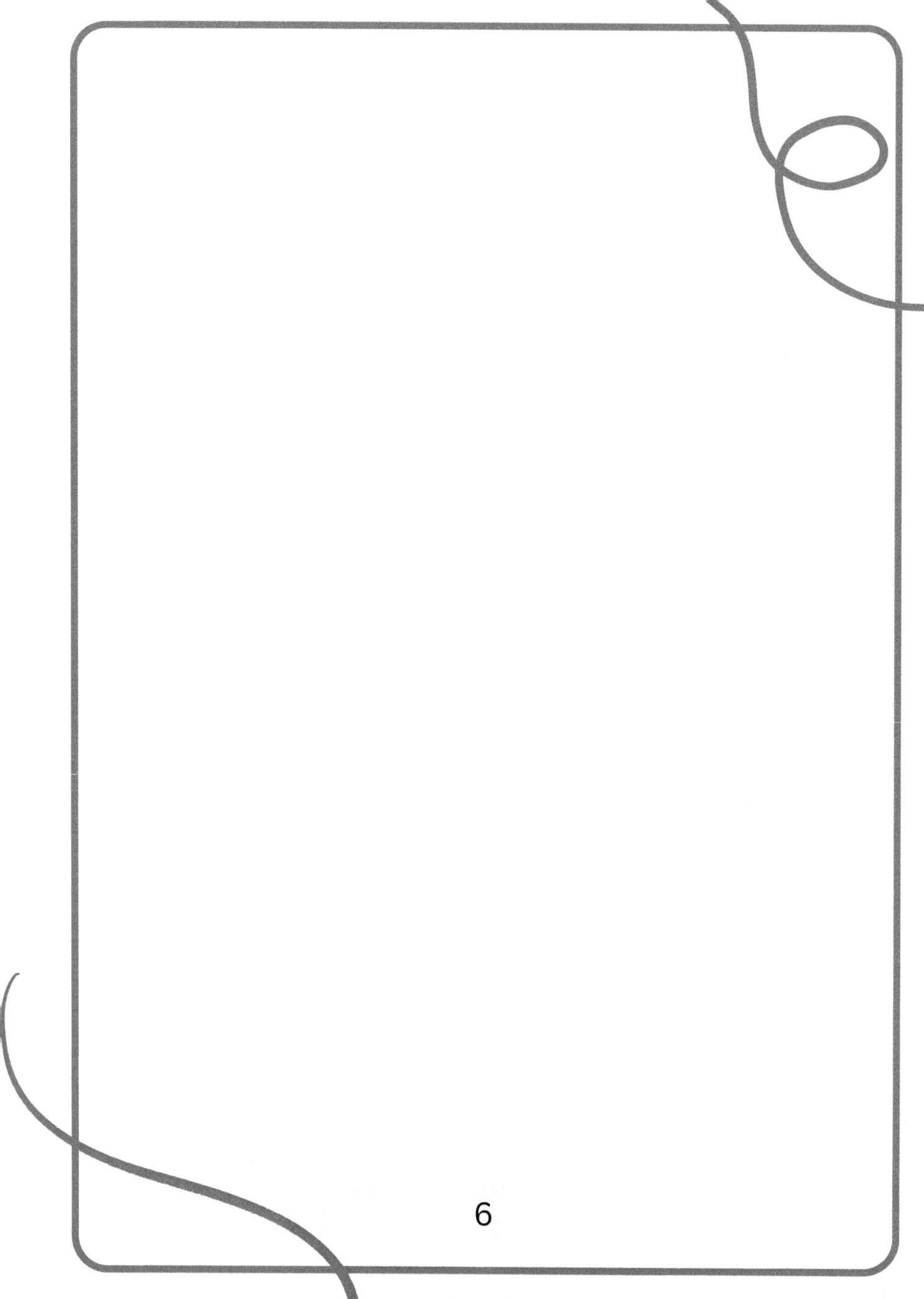

6

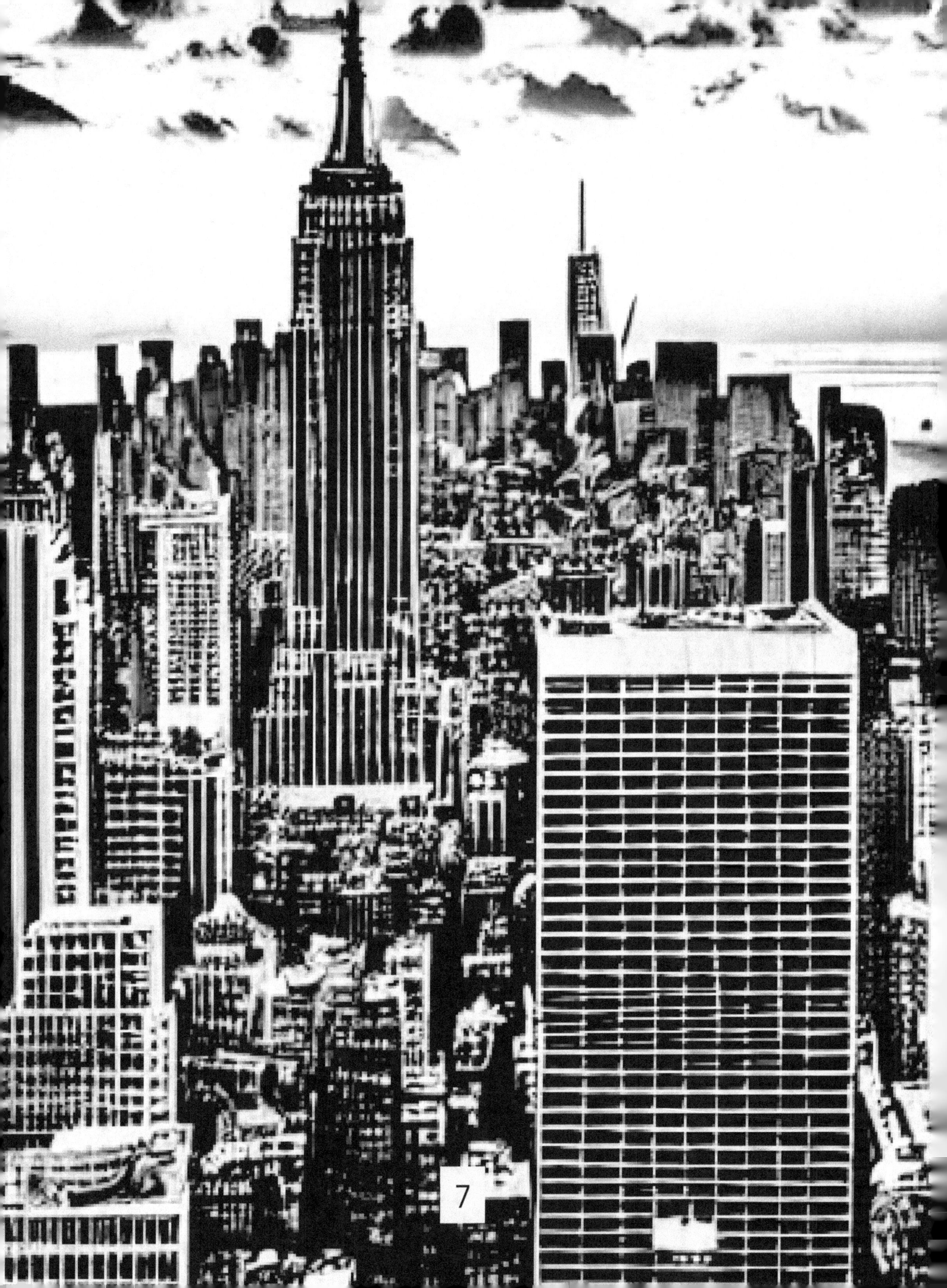

7

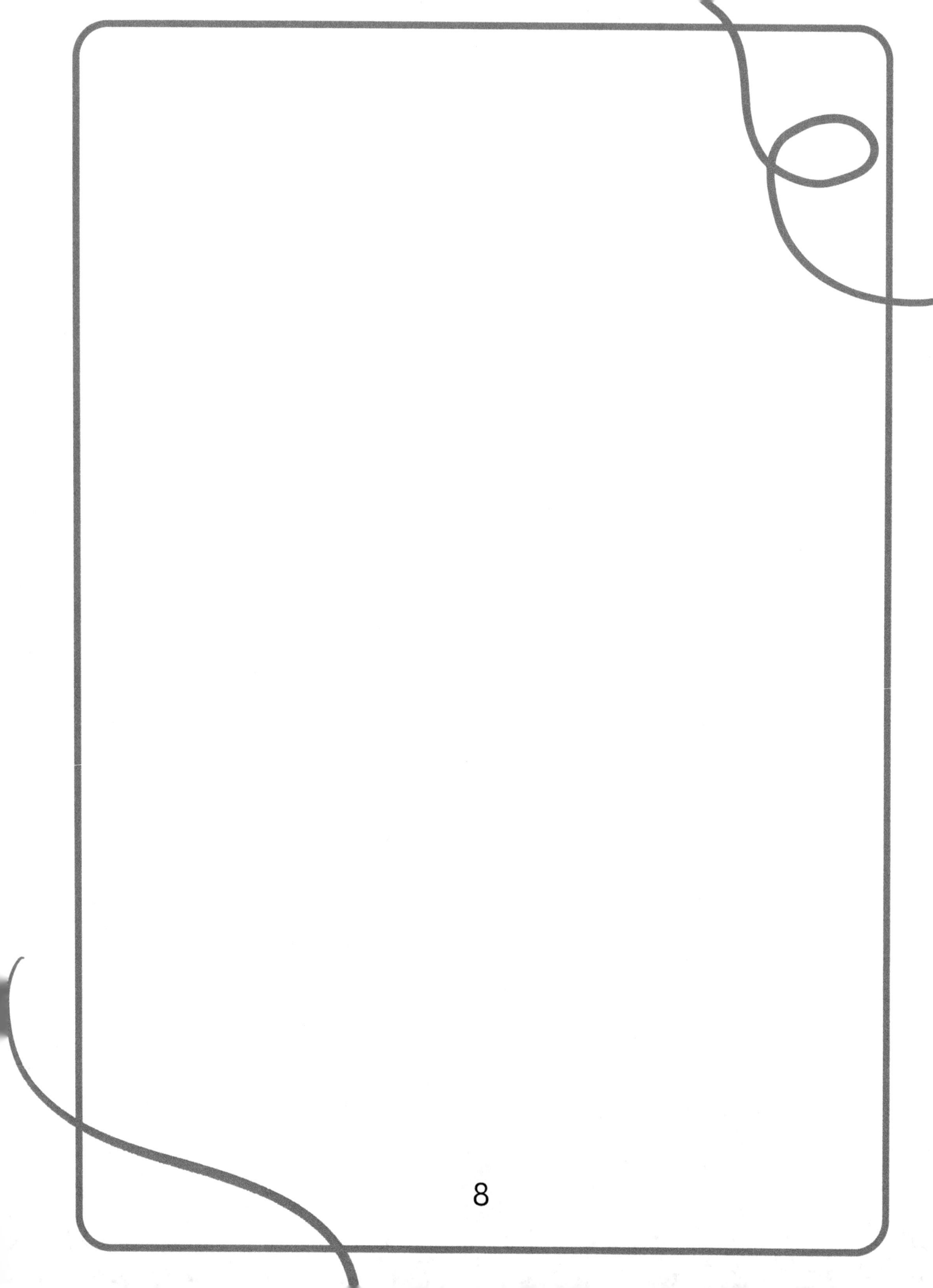

8

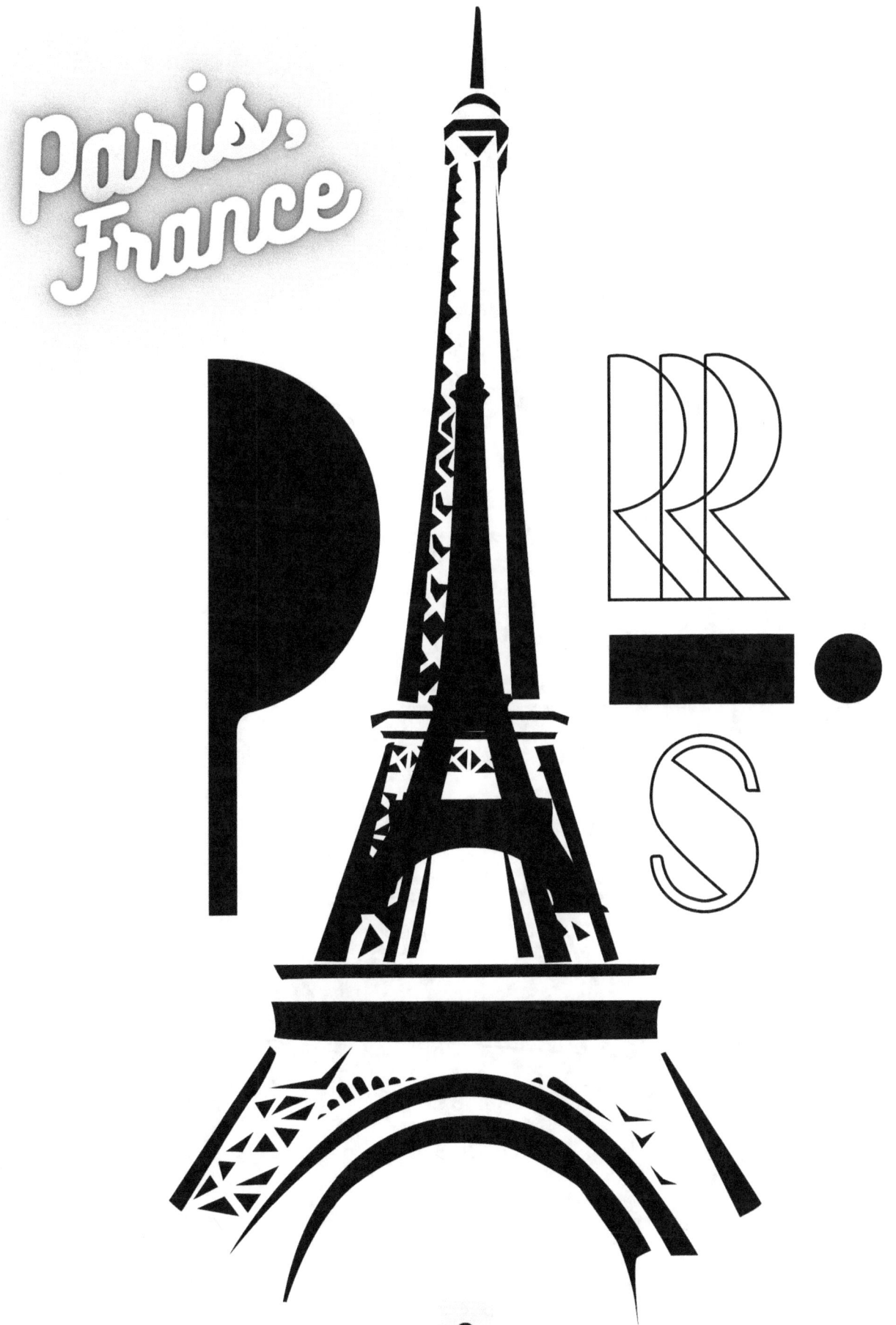

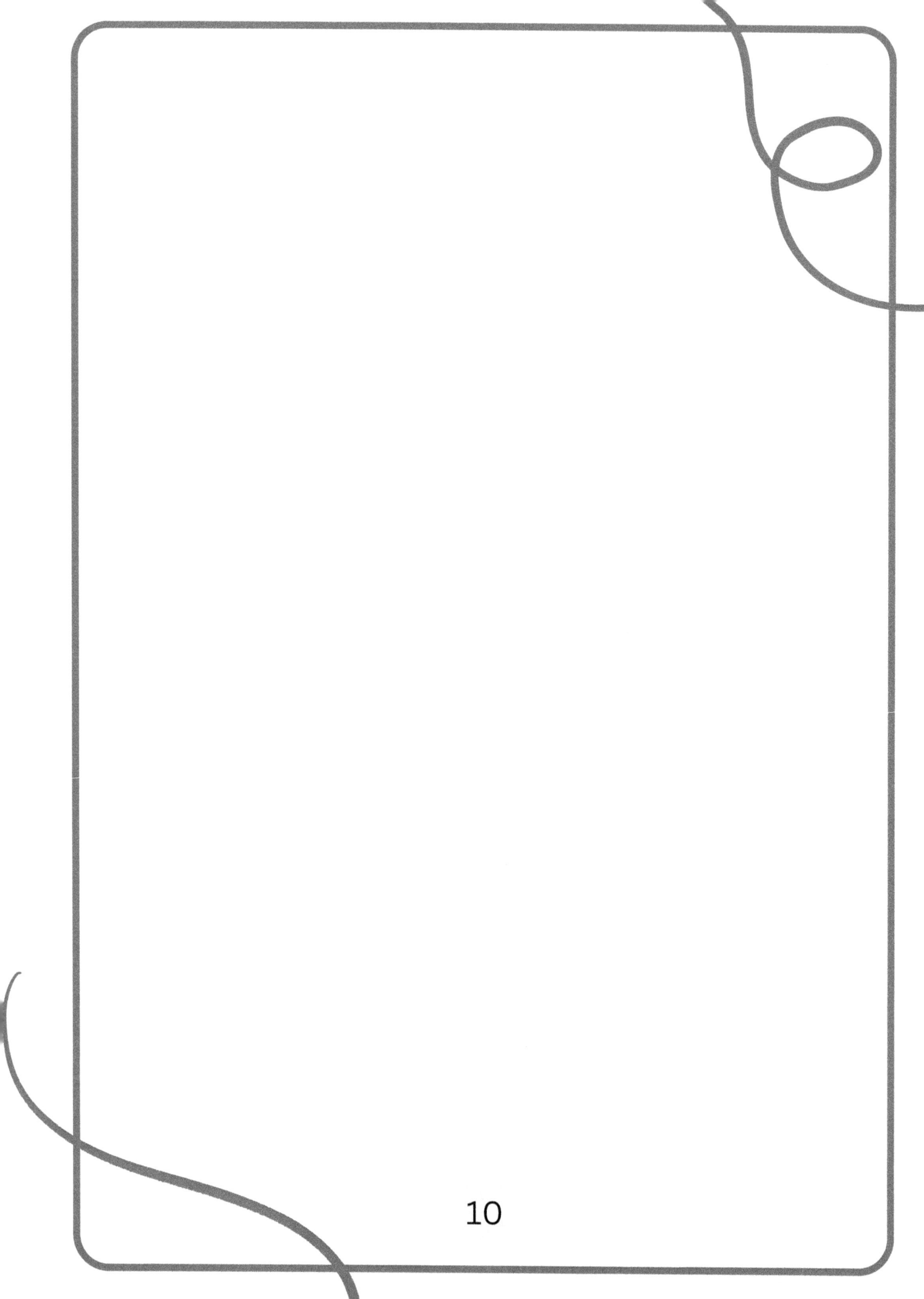

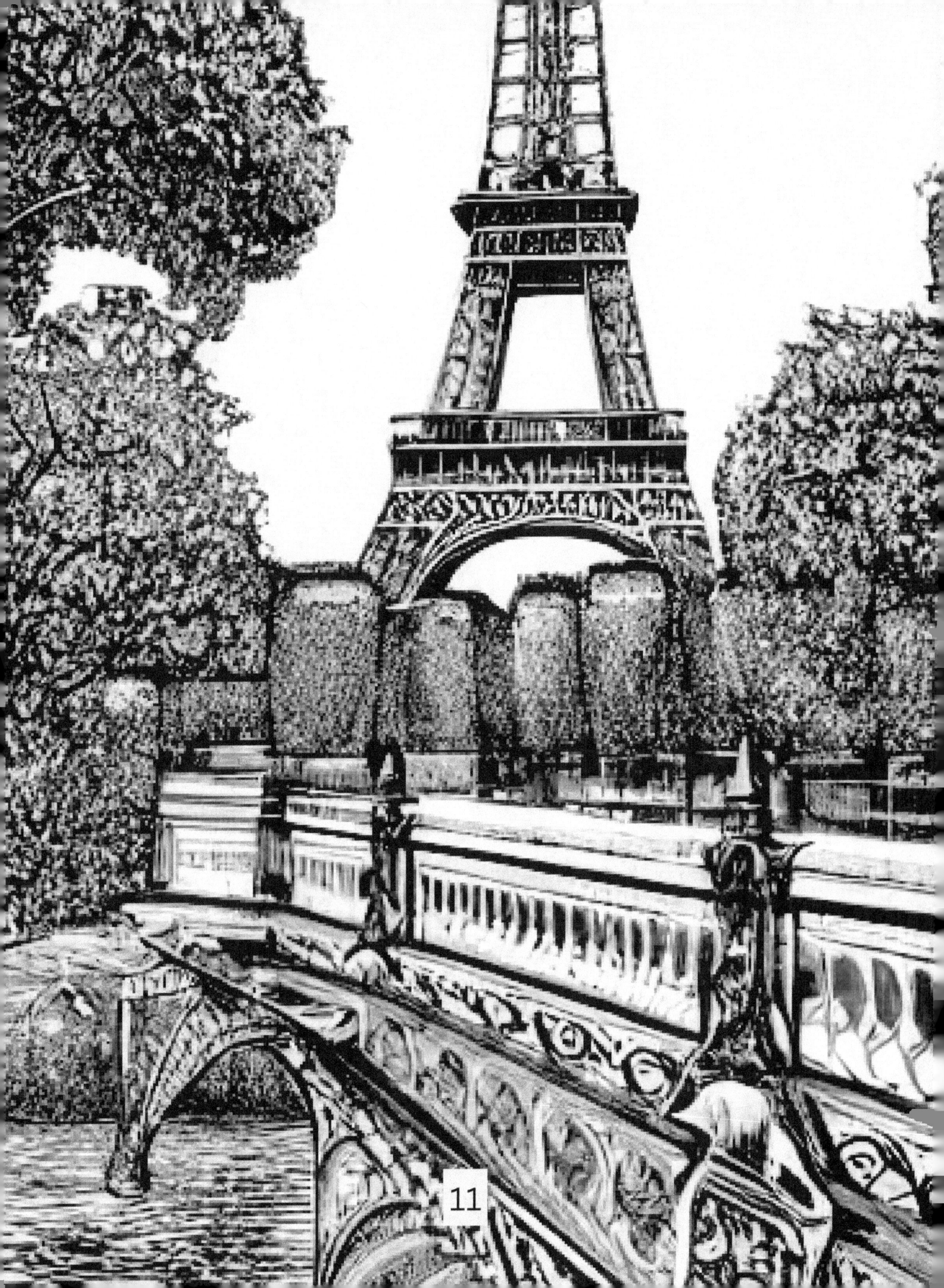

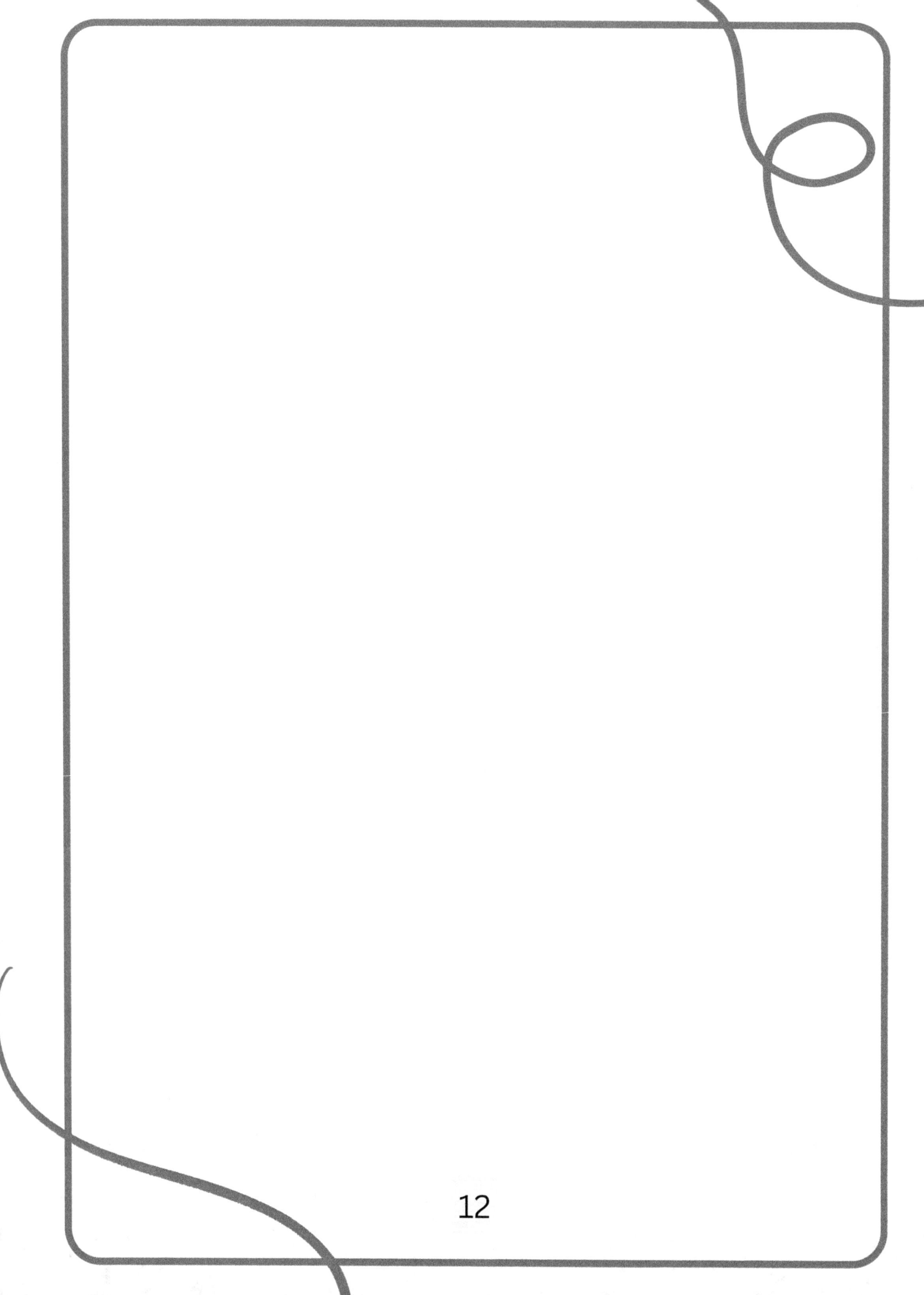

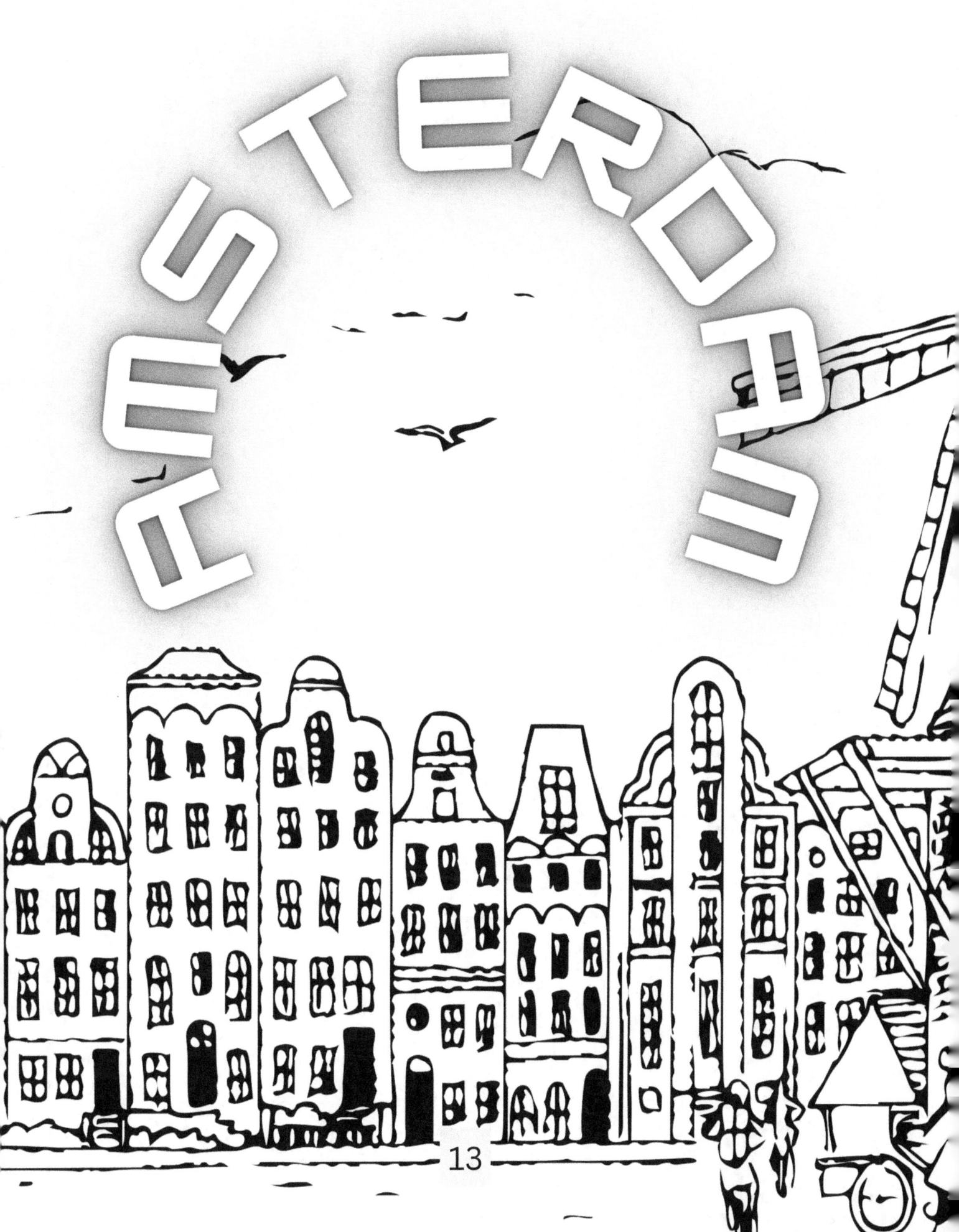

13

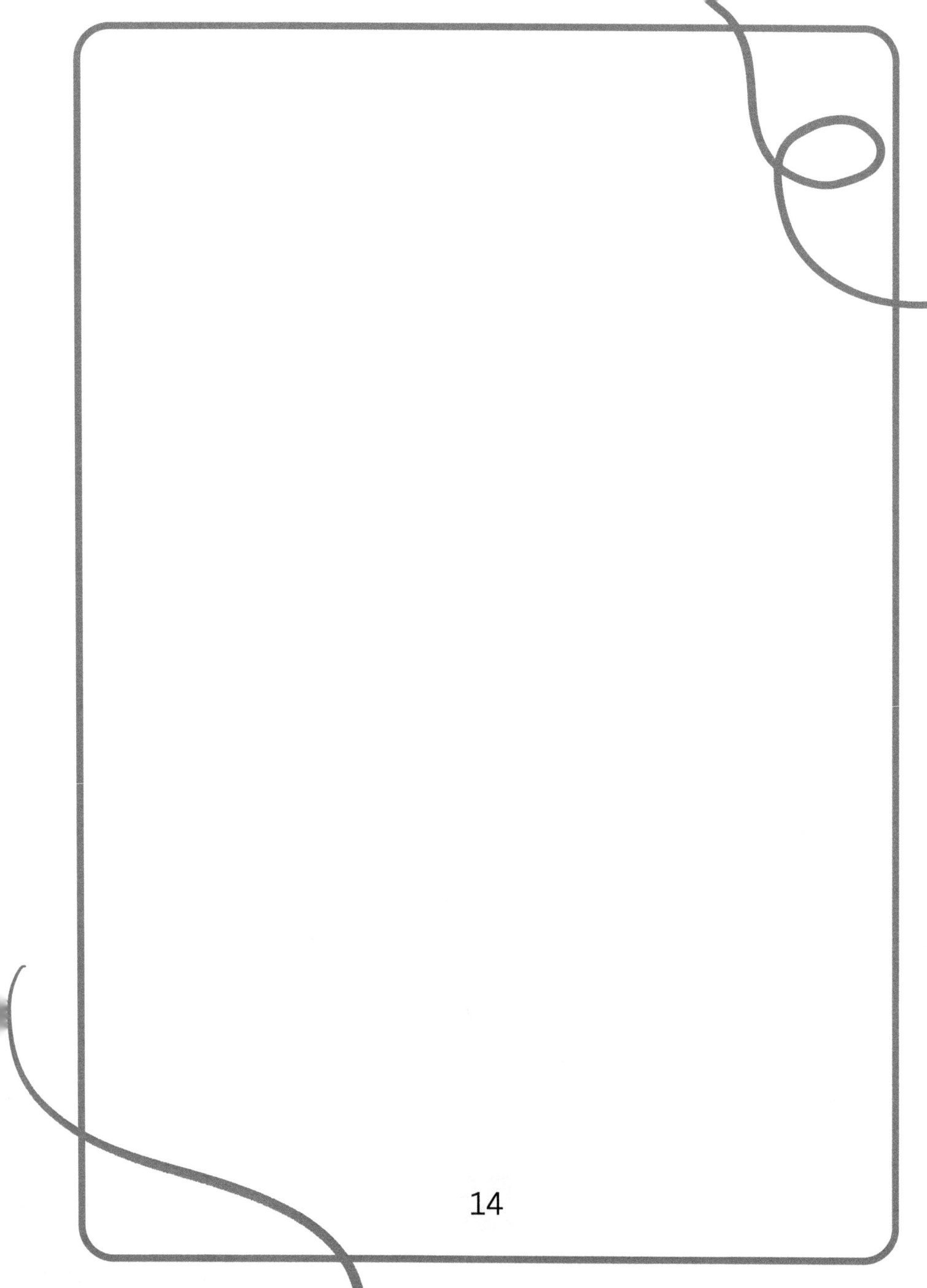

14

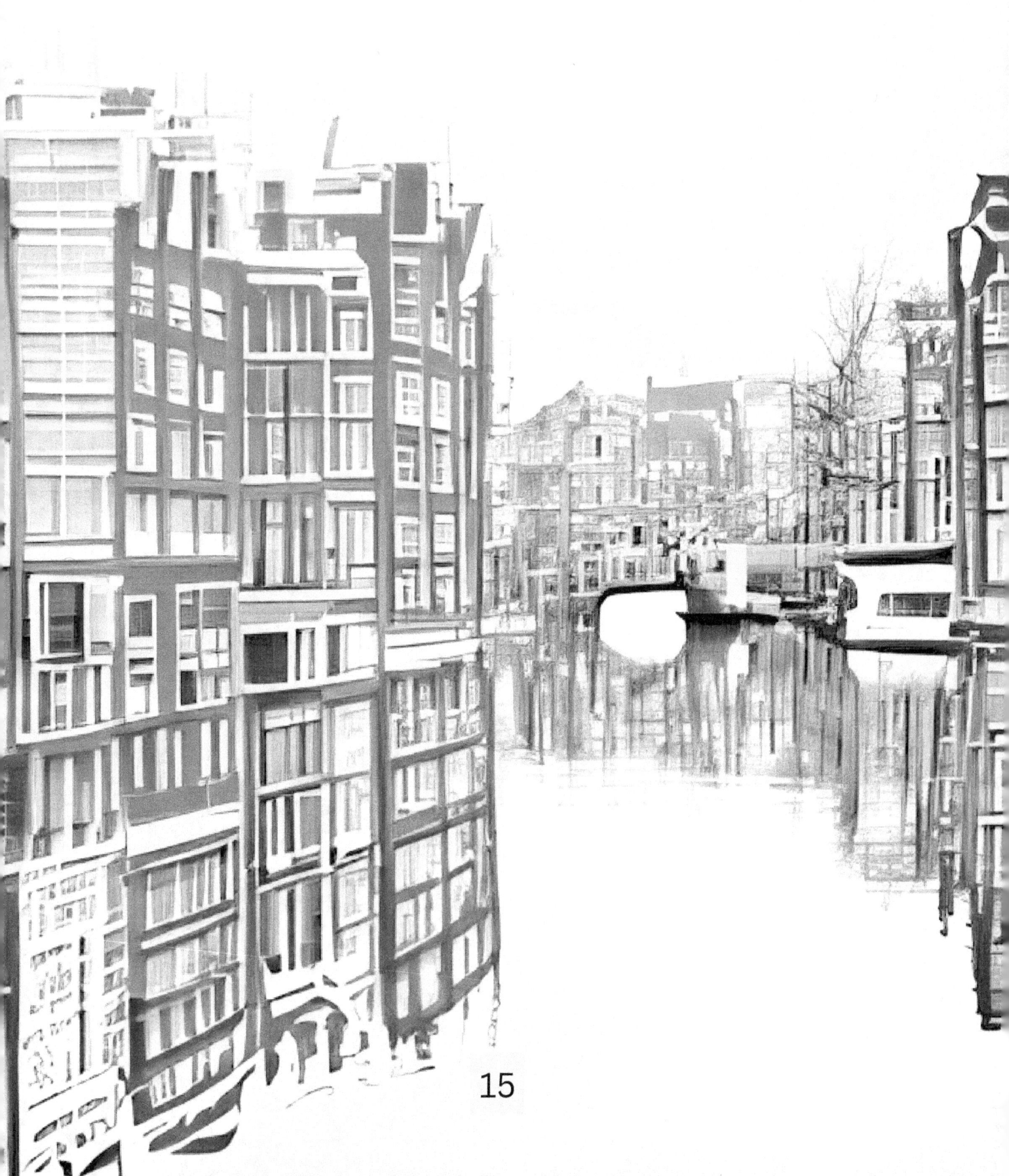

15

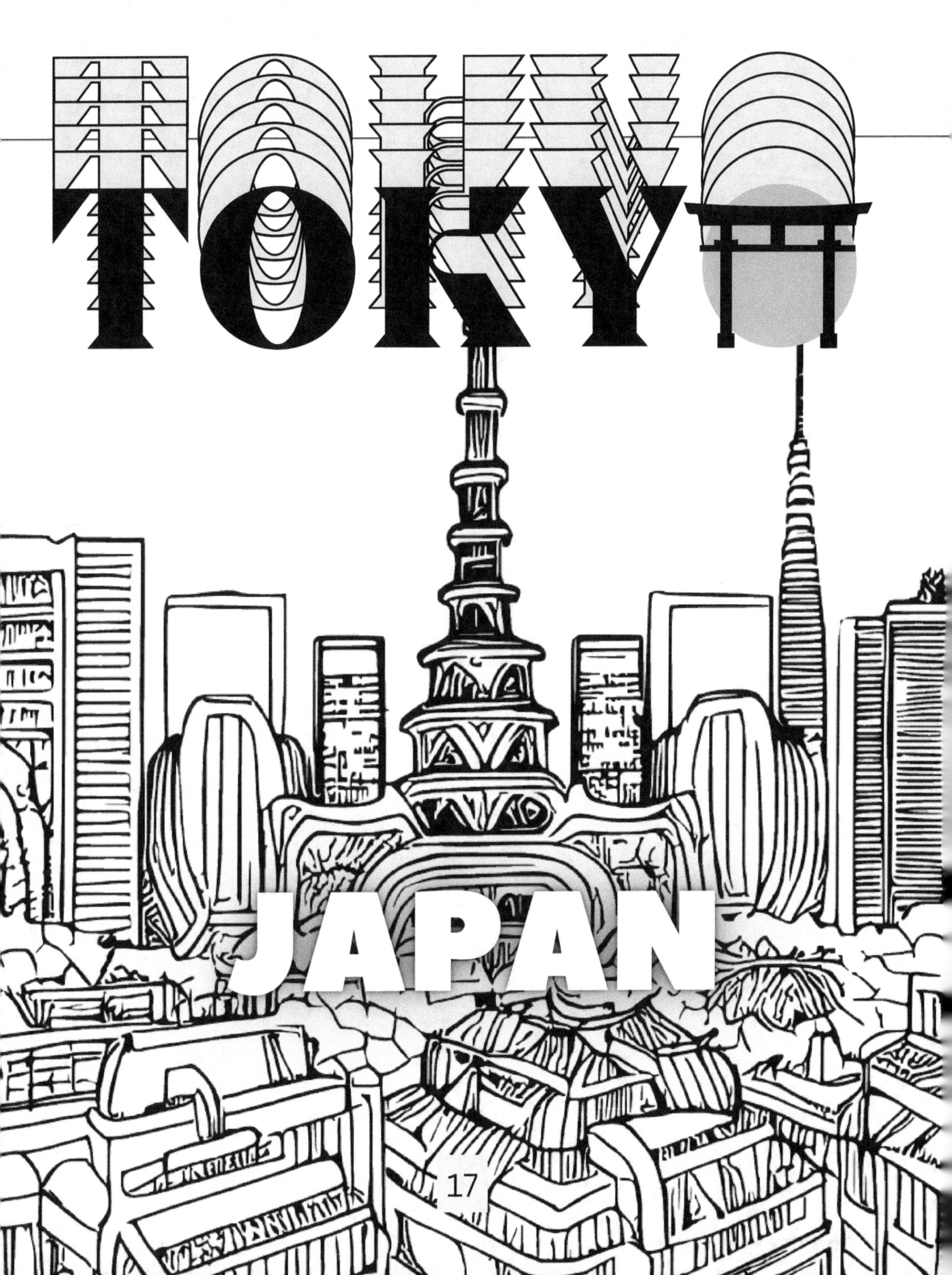

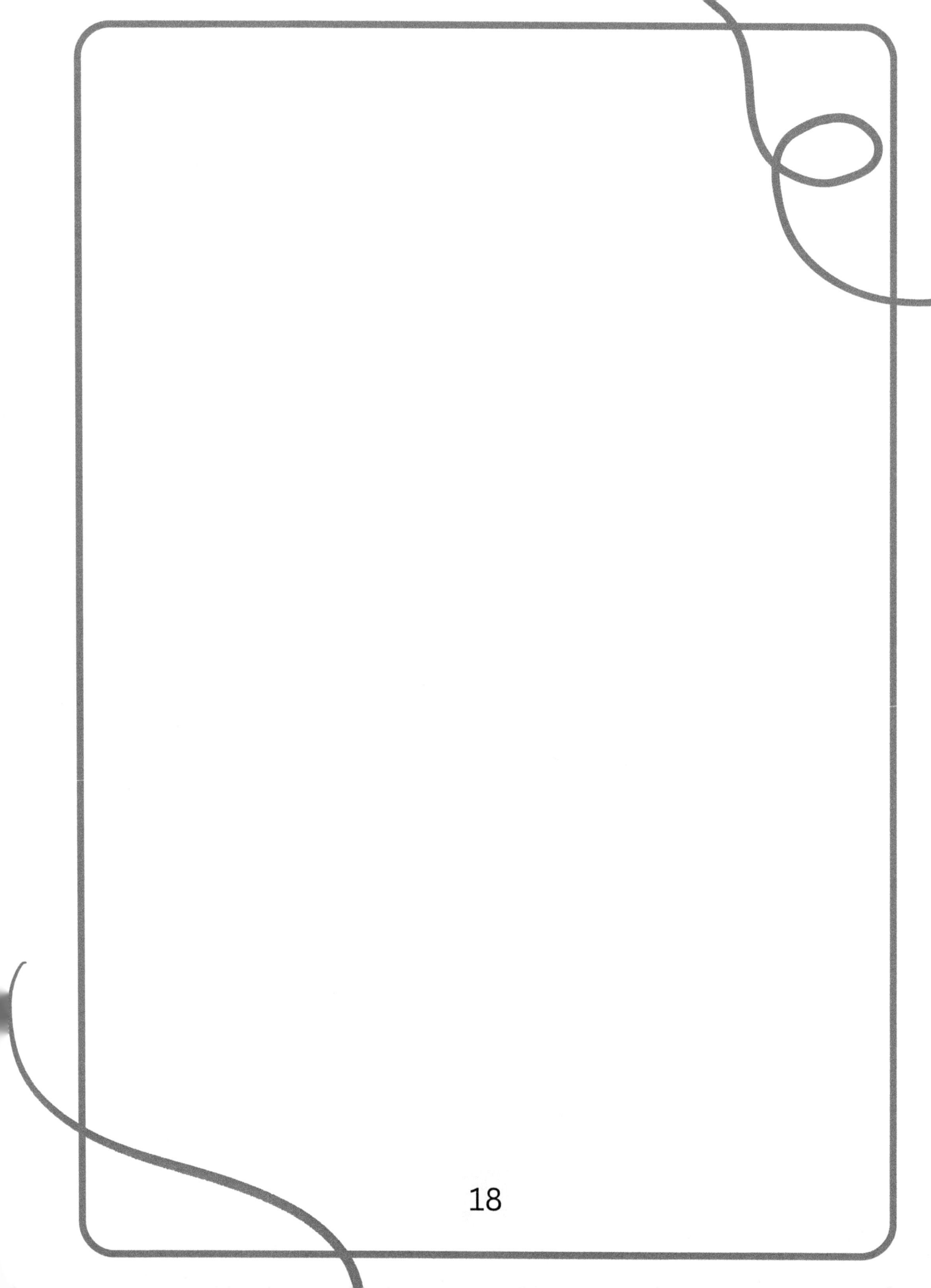

18

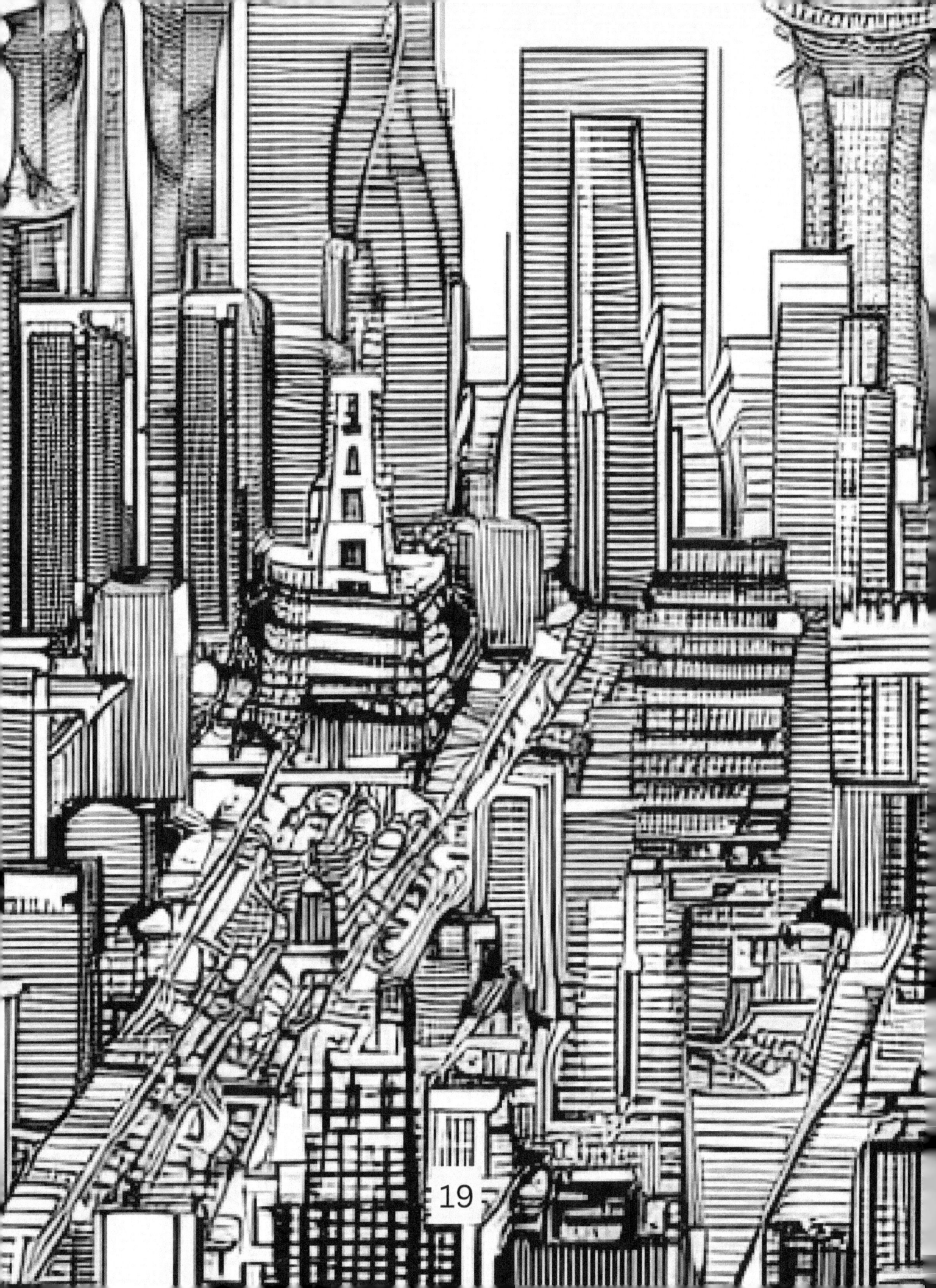
19

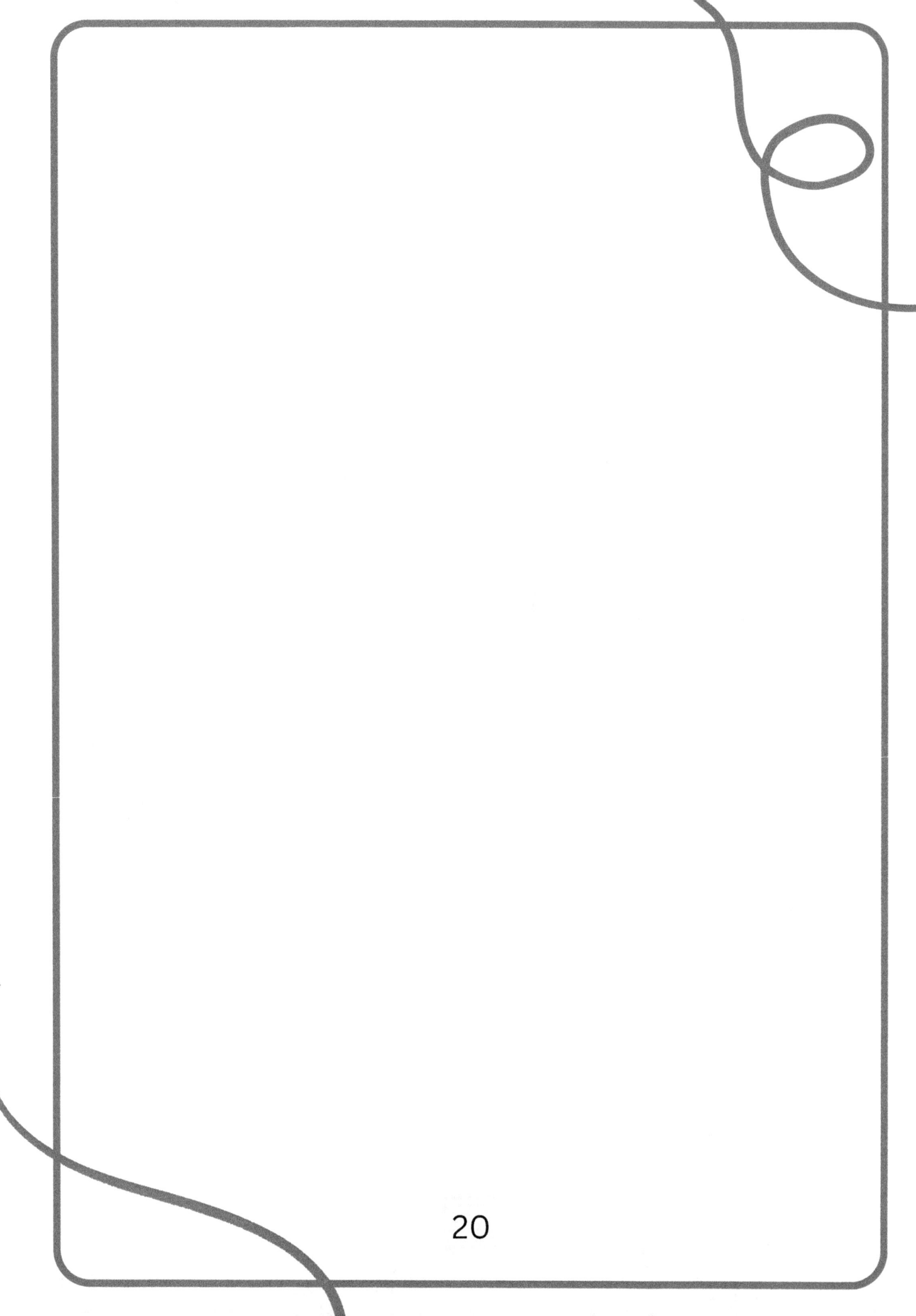

20

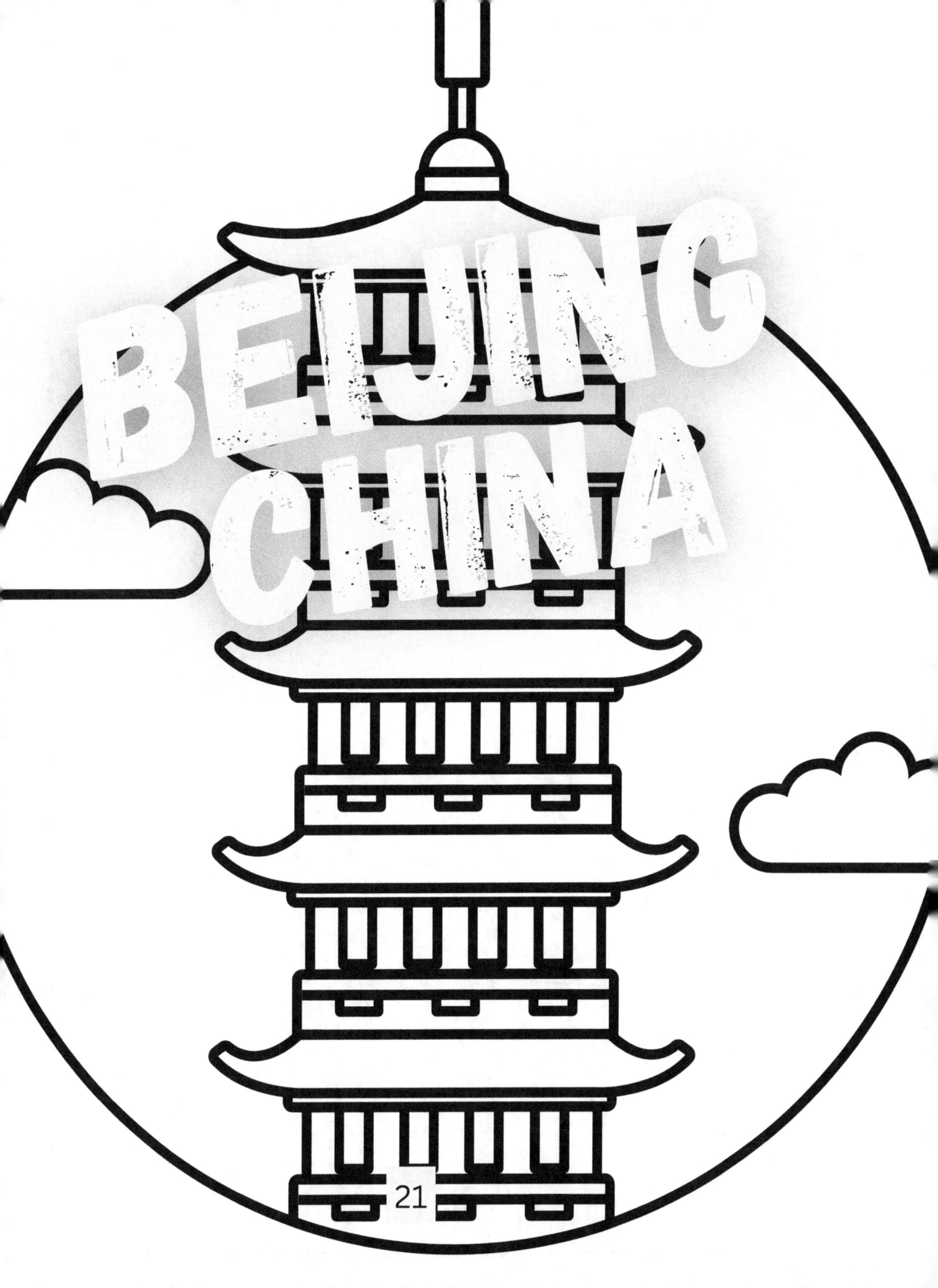

21

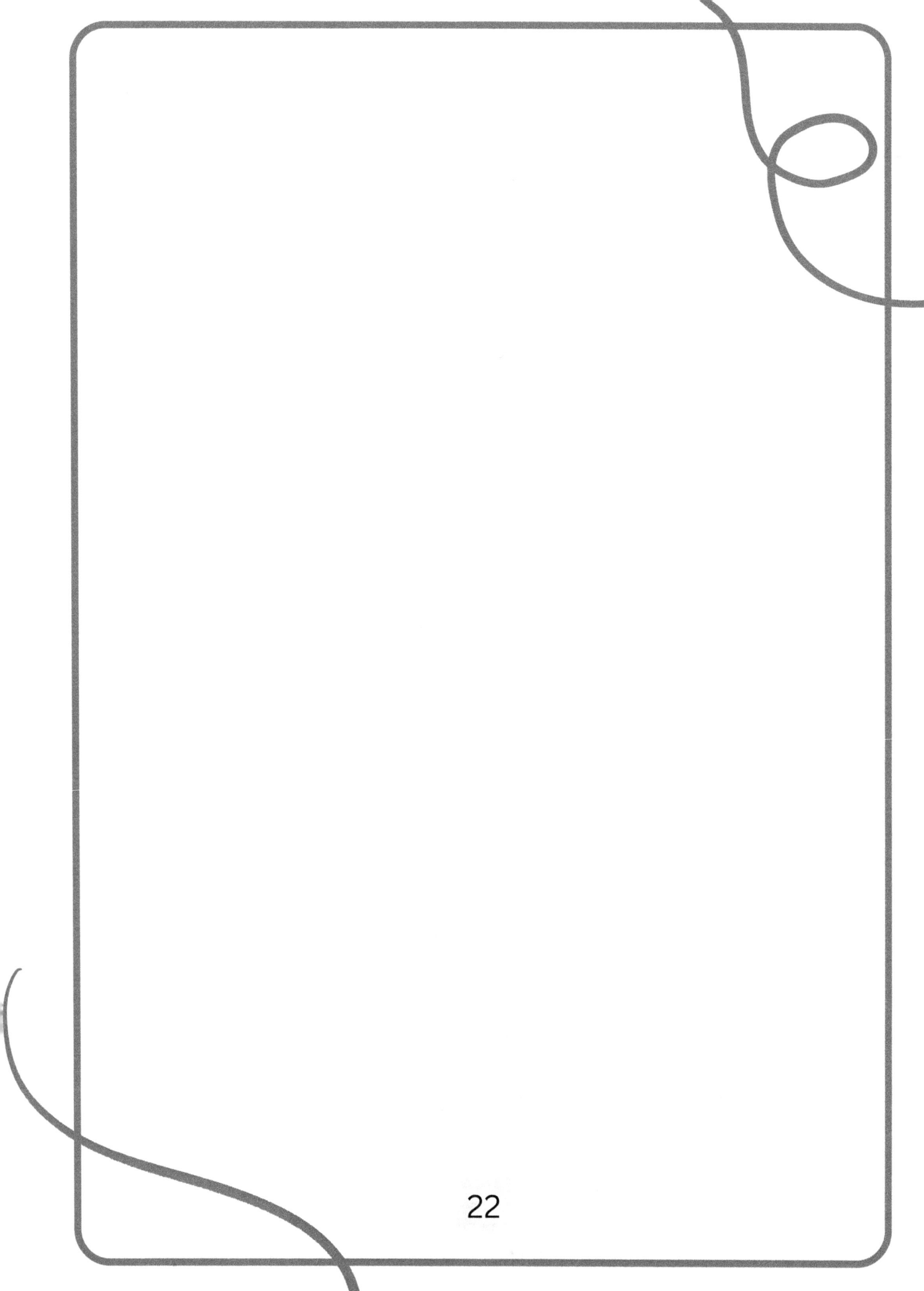

22

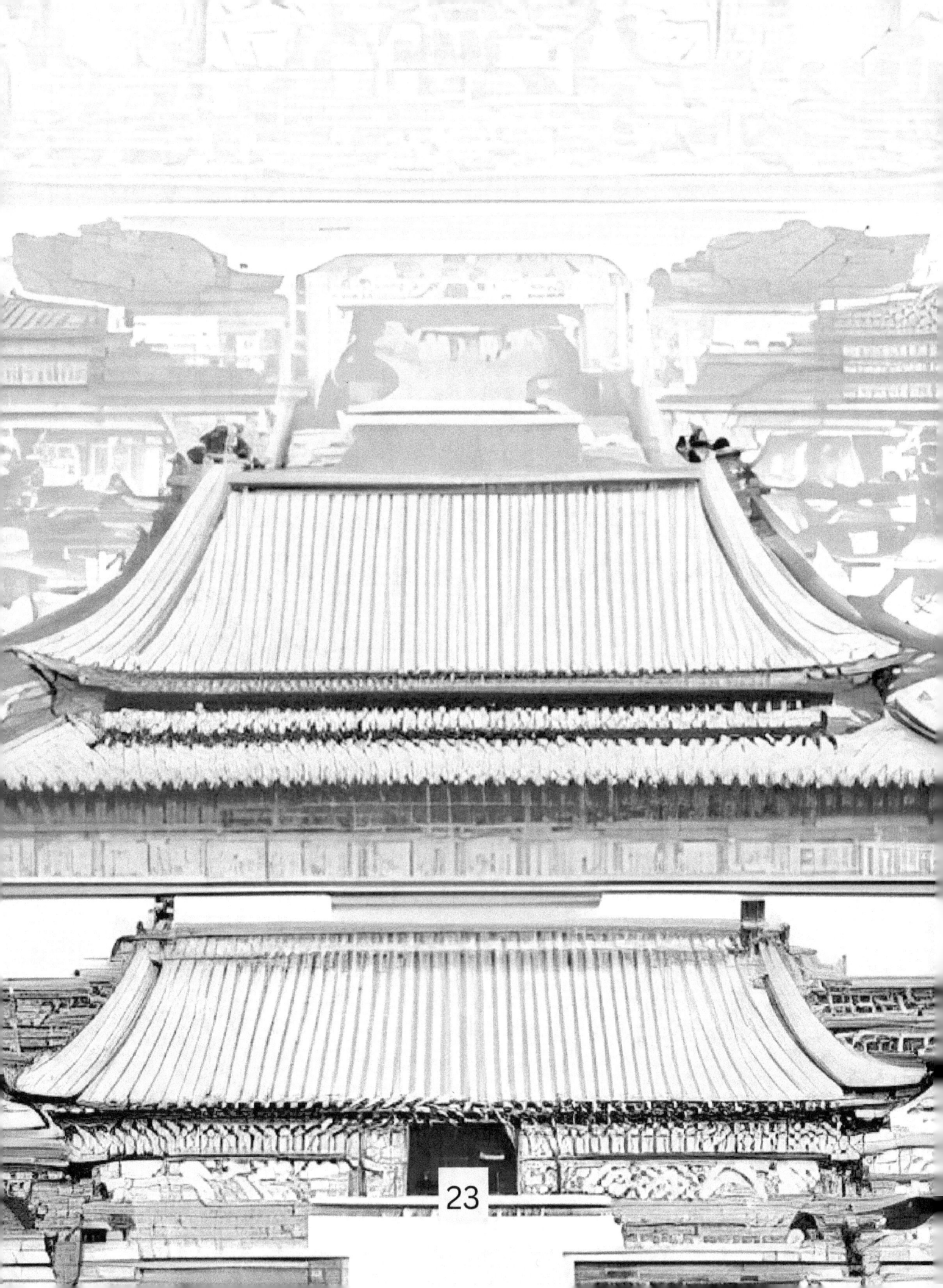

23

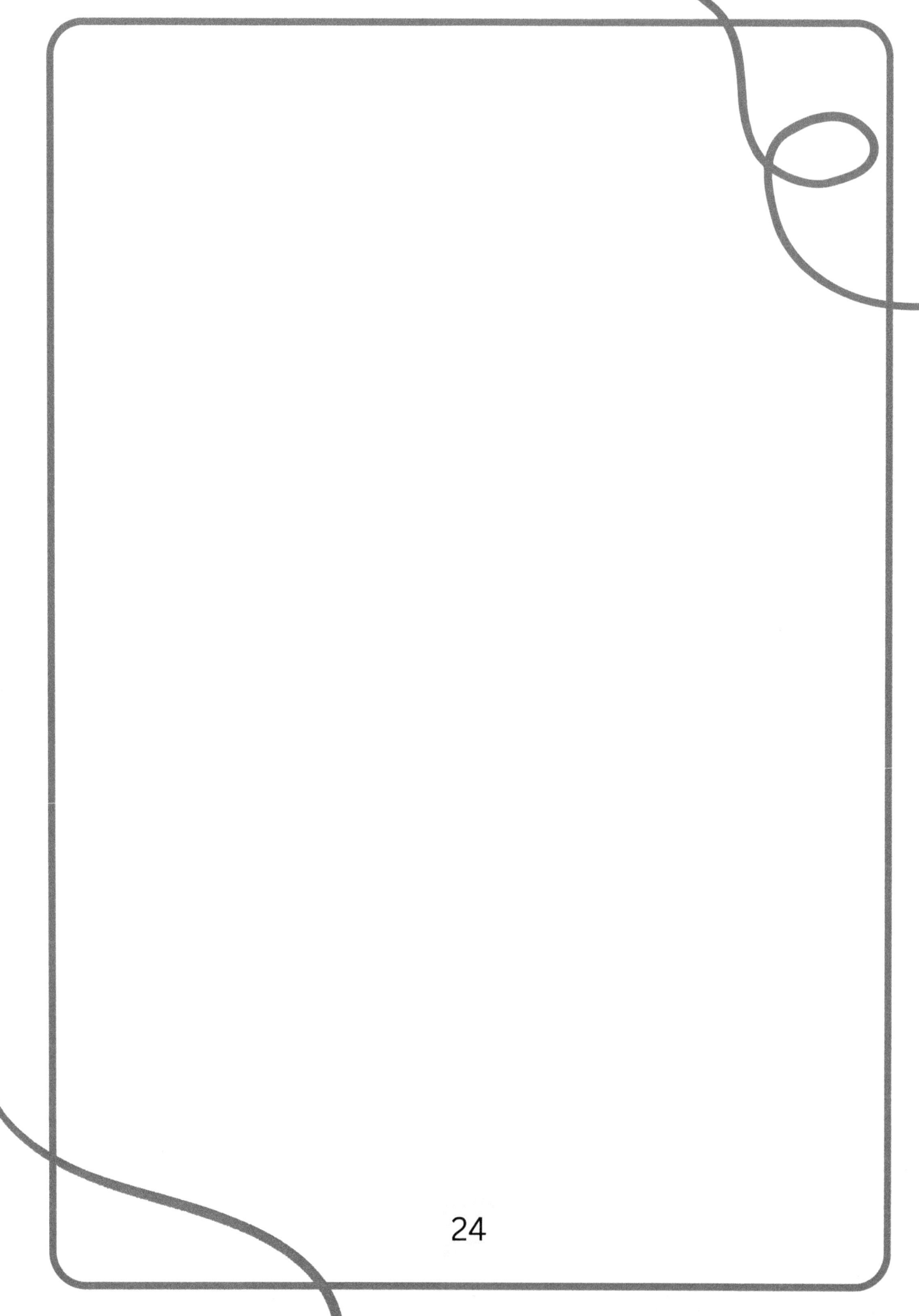

24

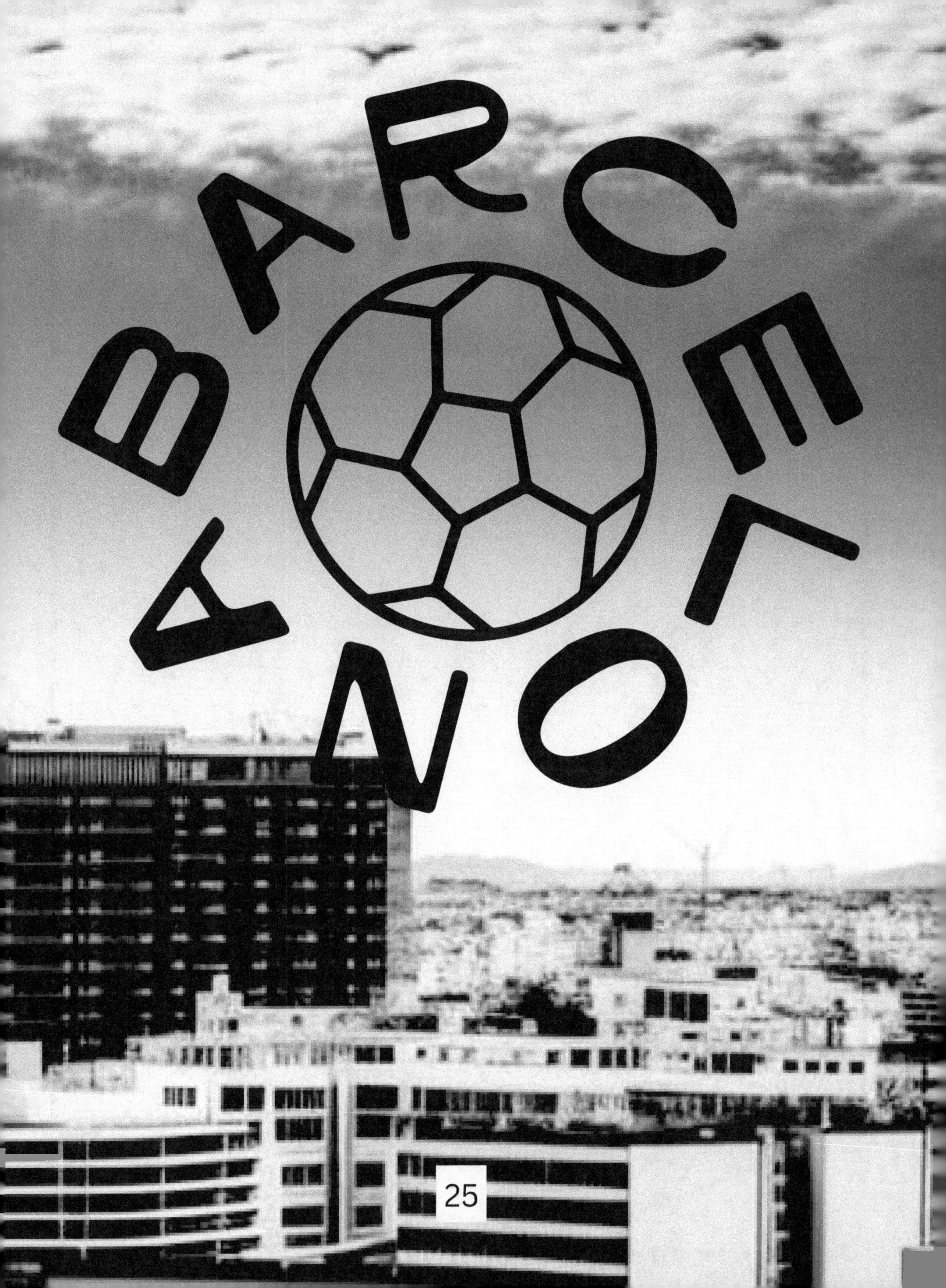
BARCELONA

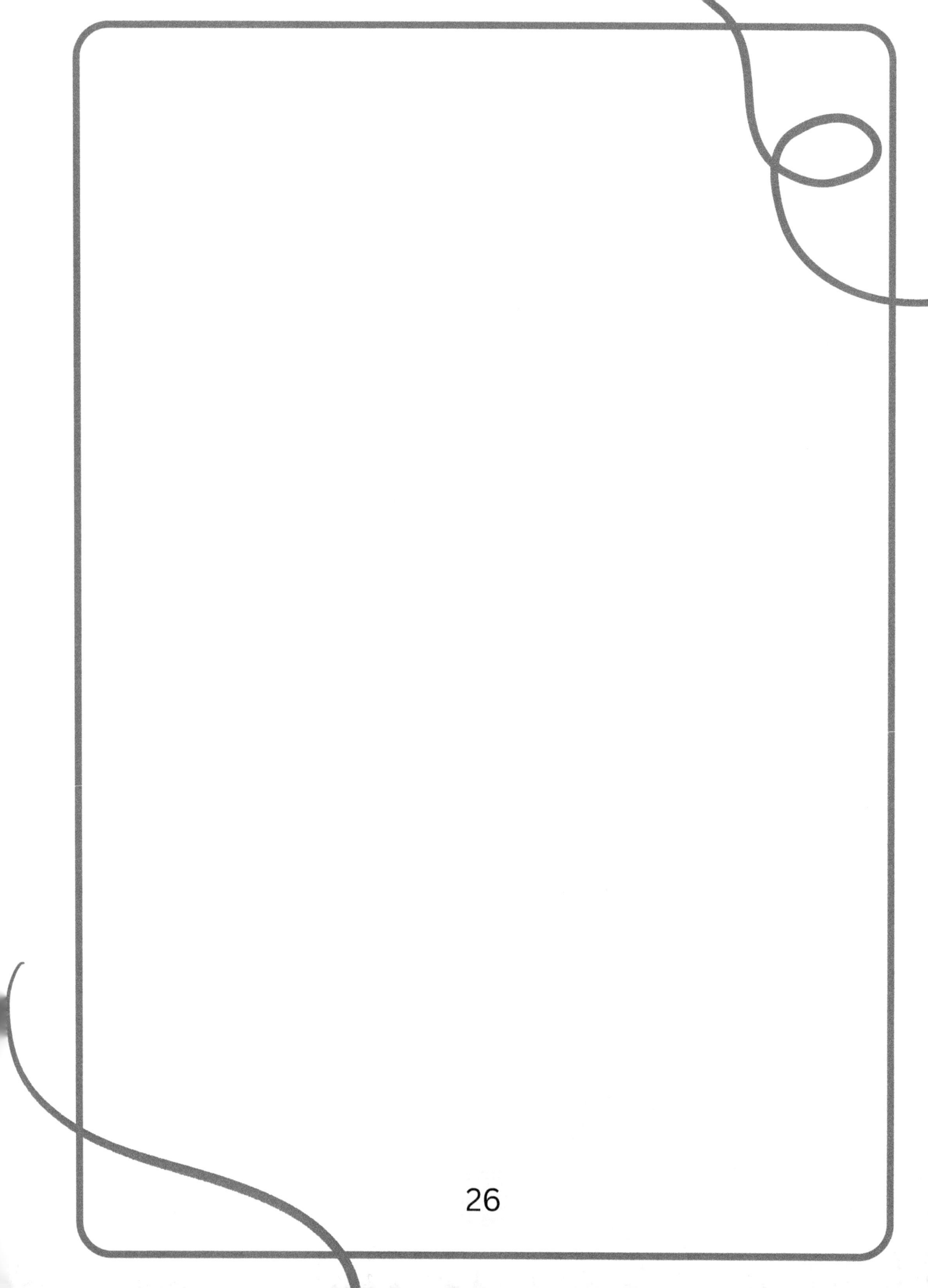

26

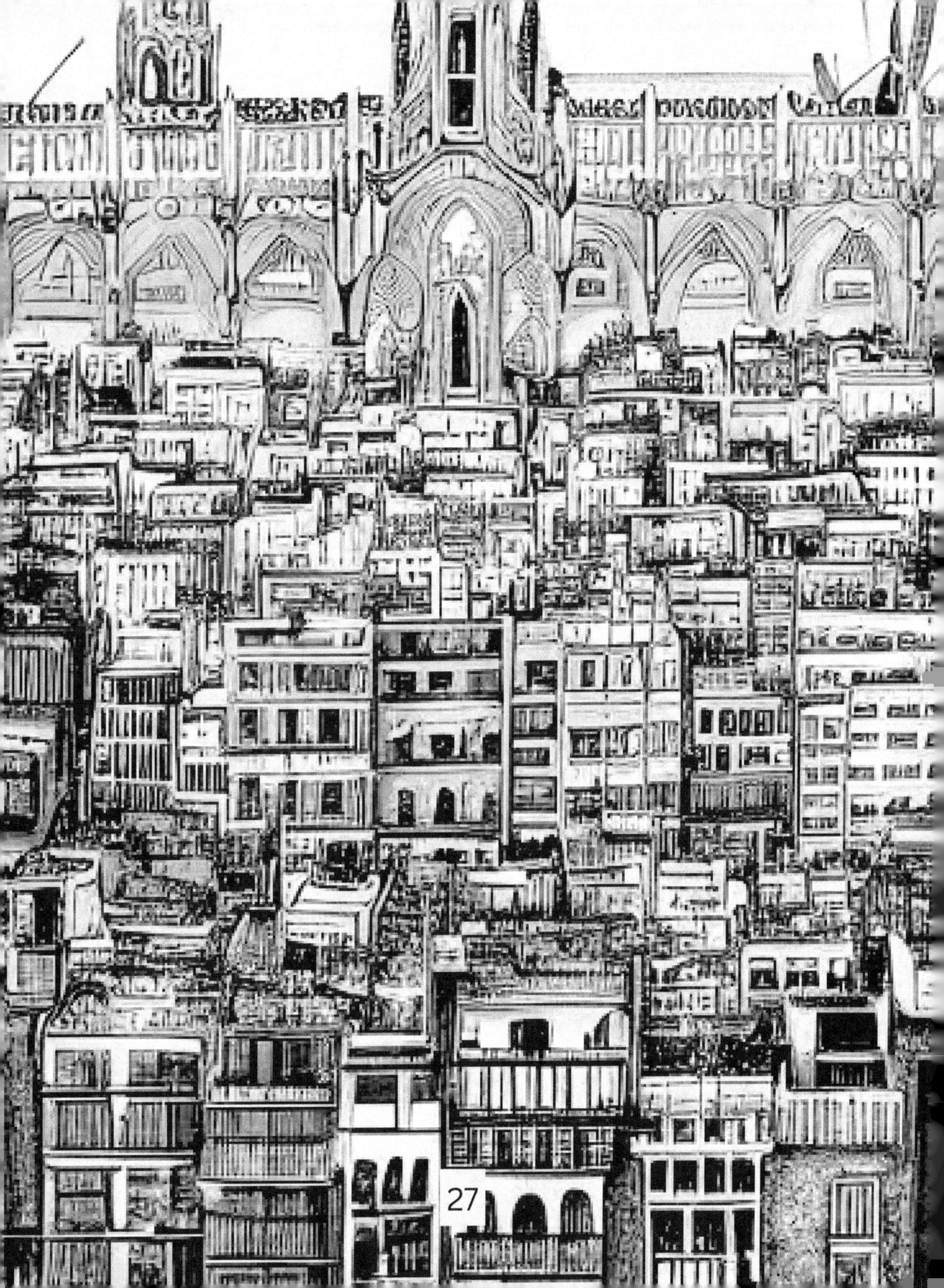

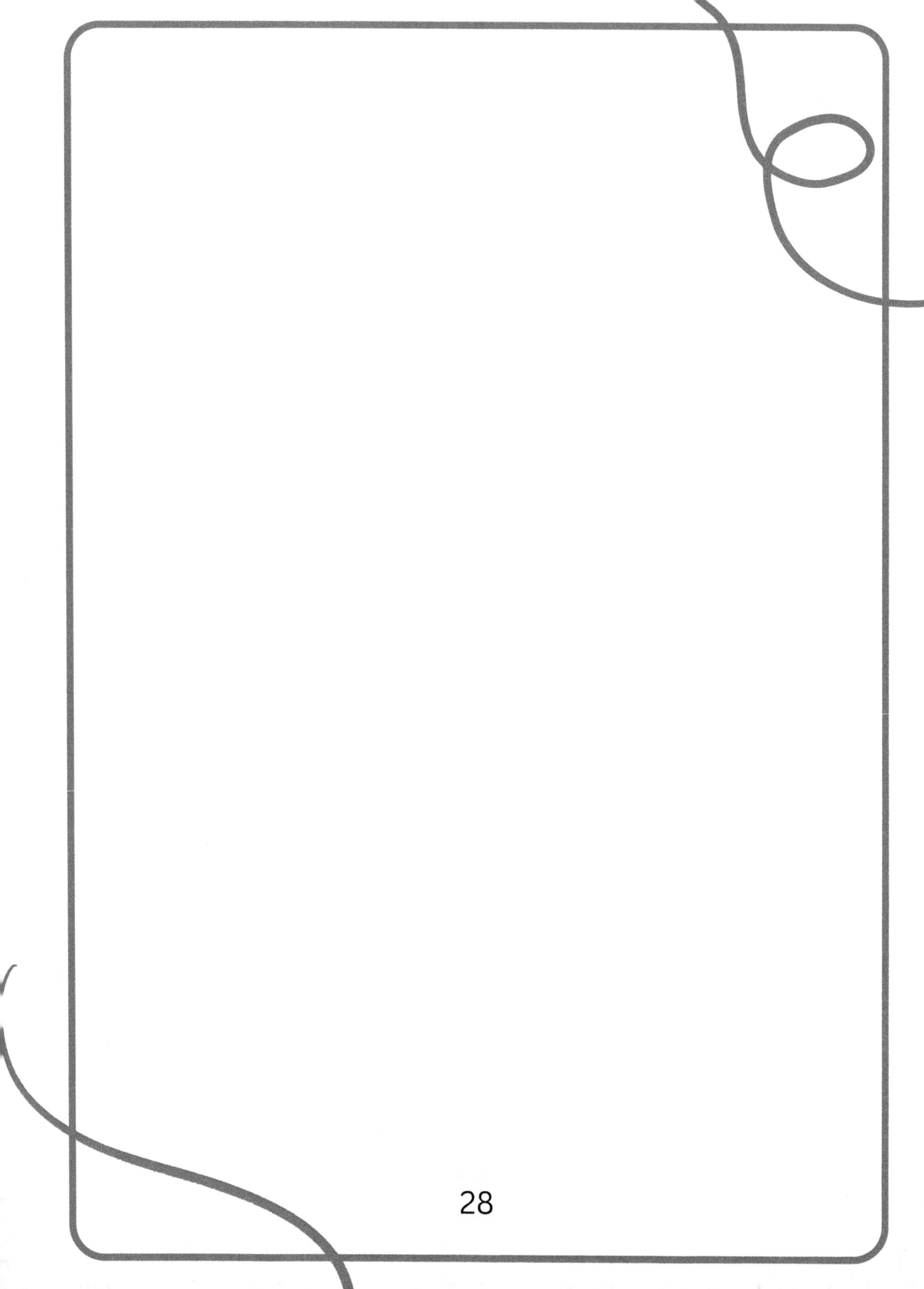

28

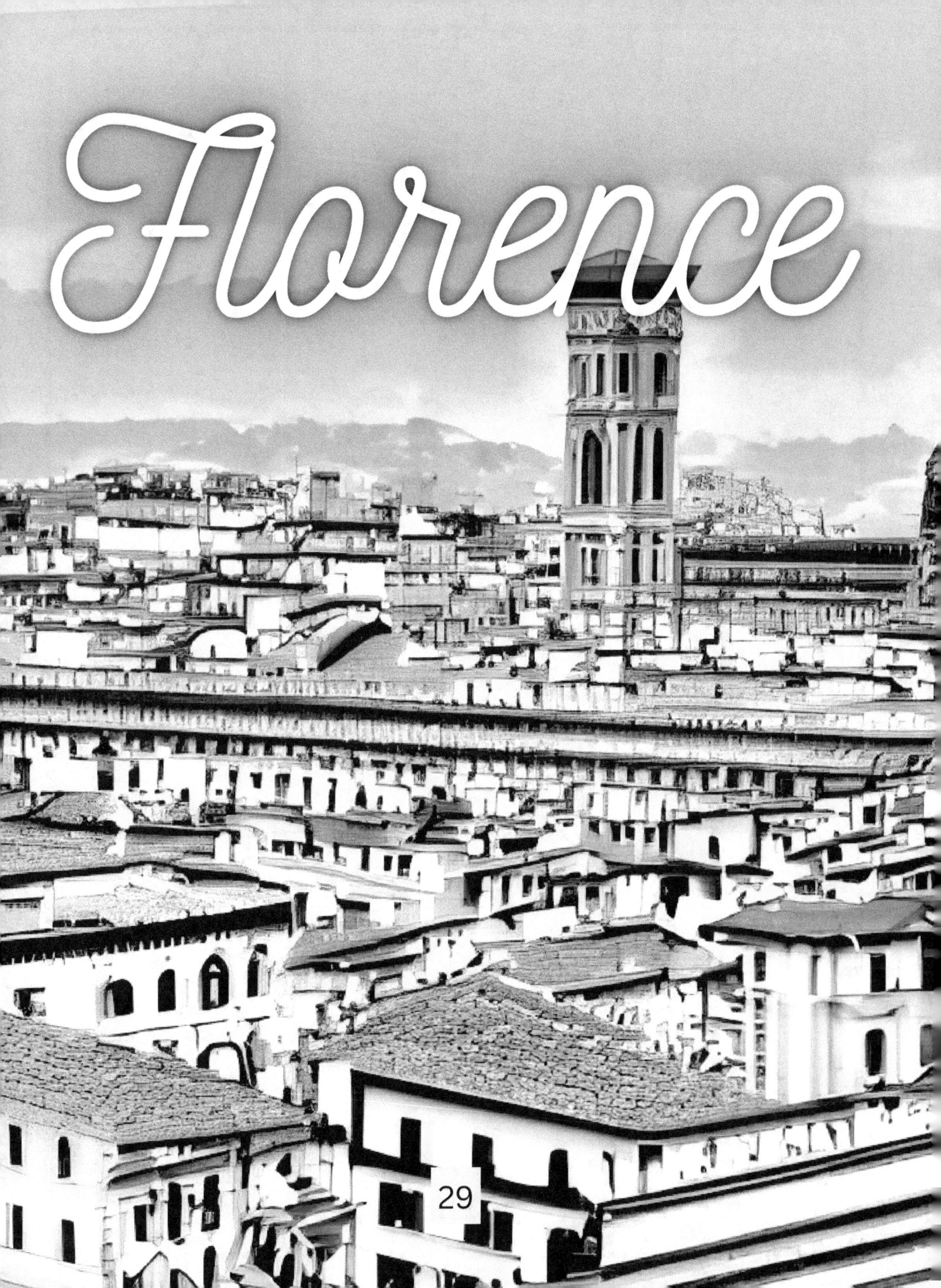

Florence

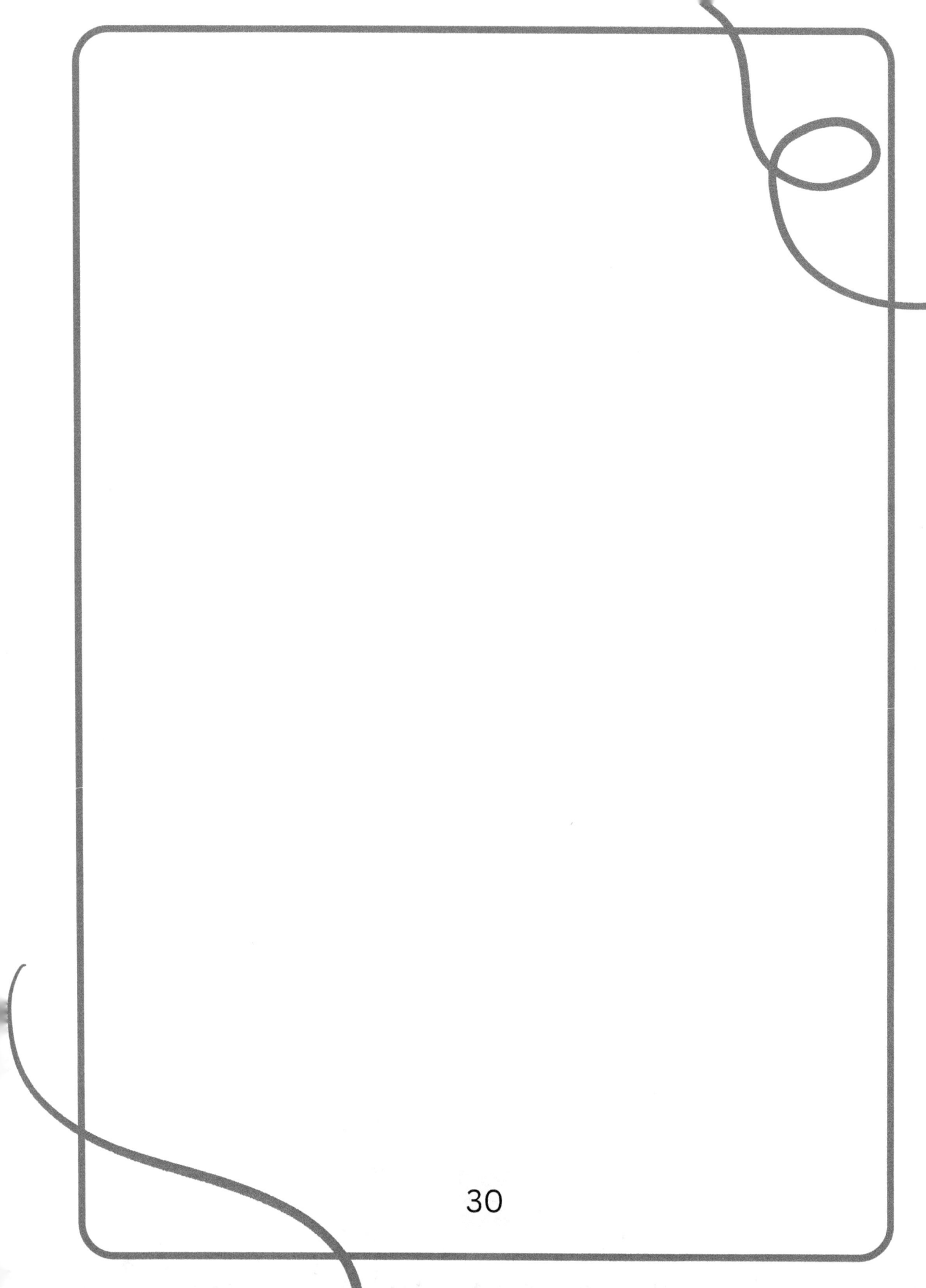

30

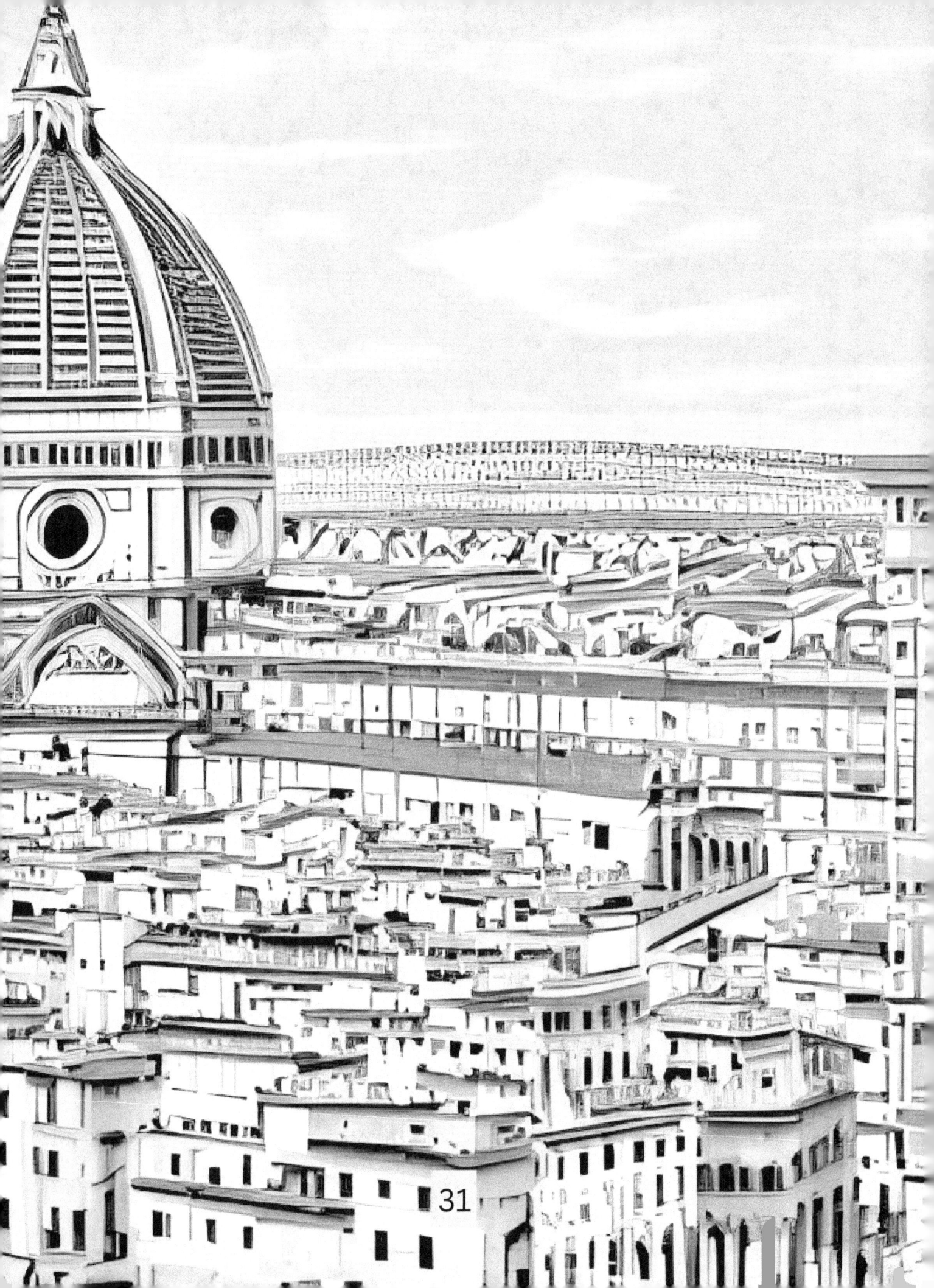

31

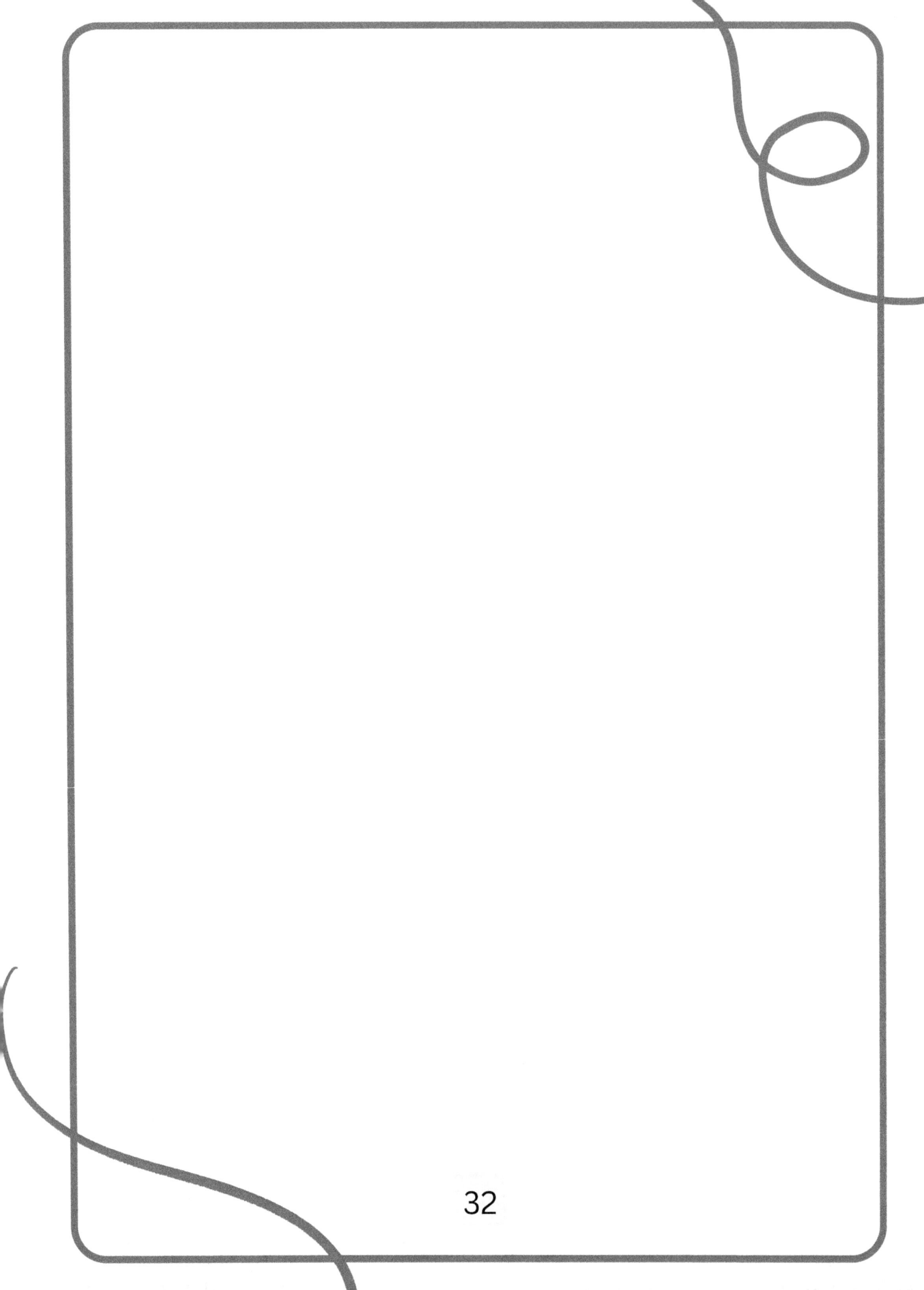

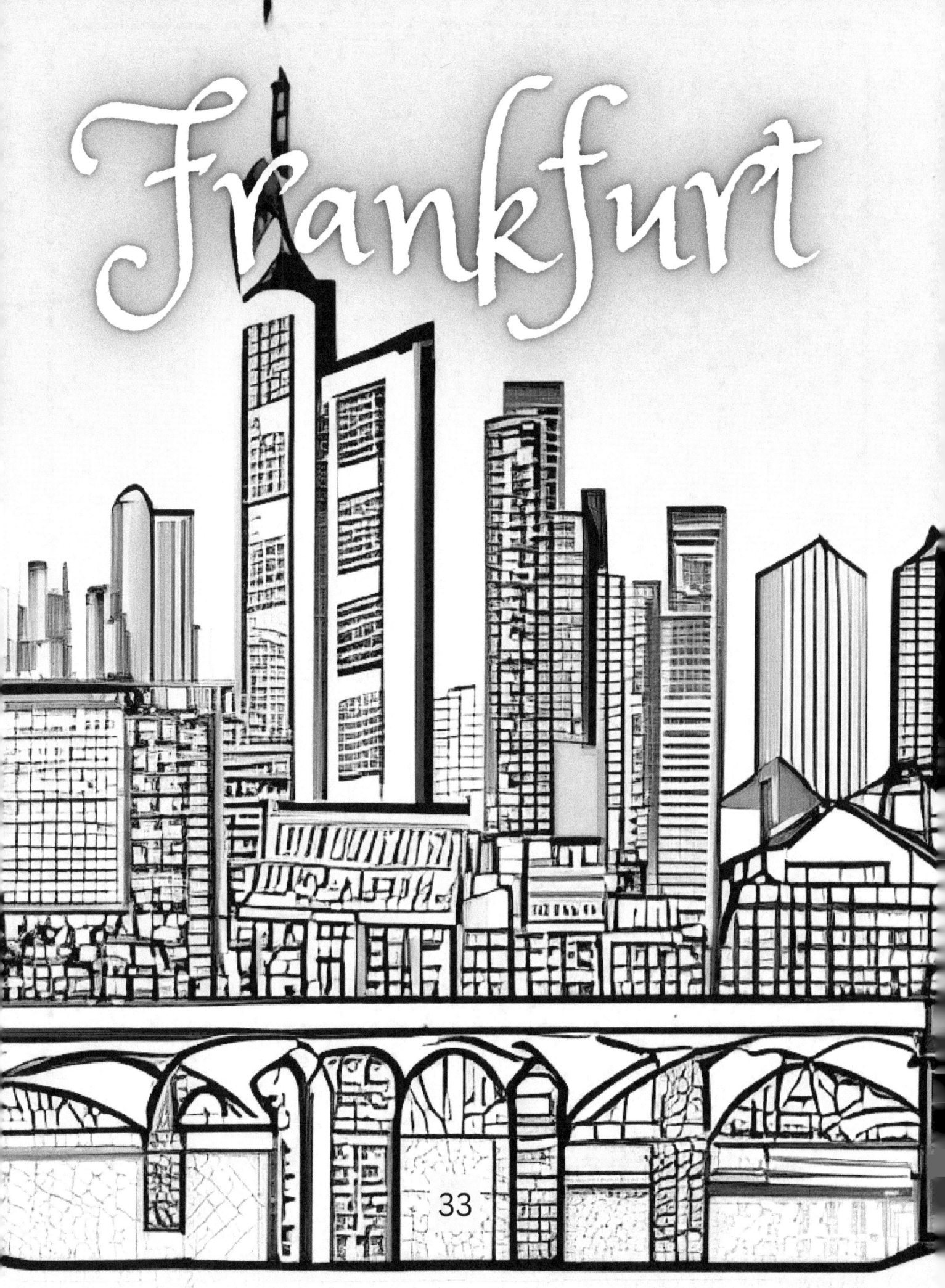

Frankfurt

33

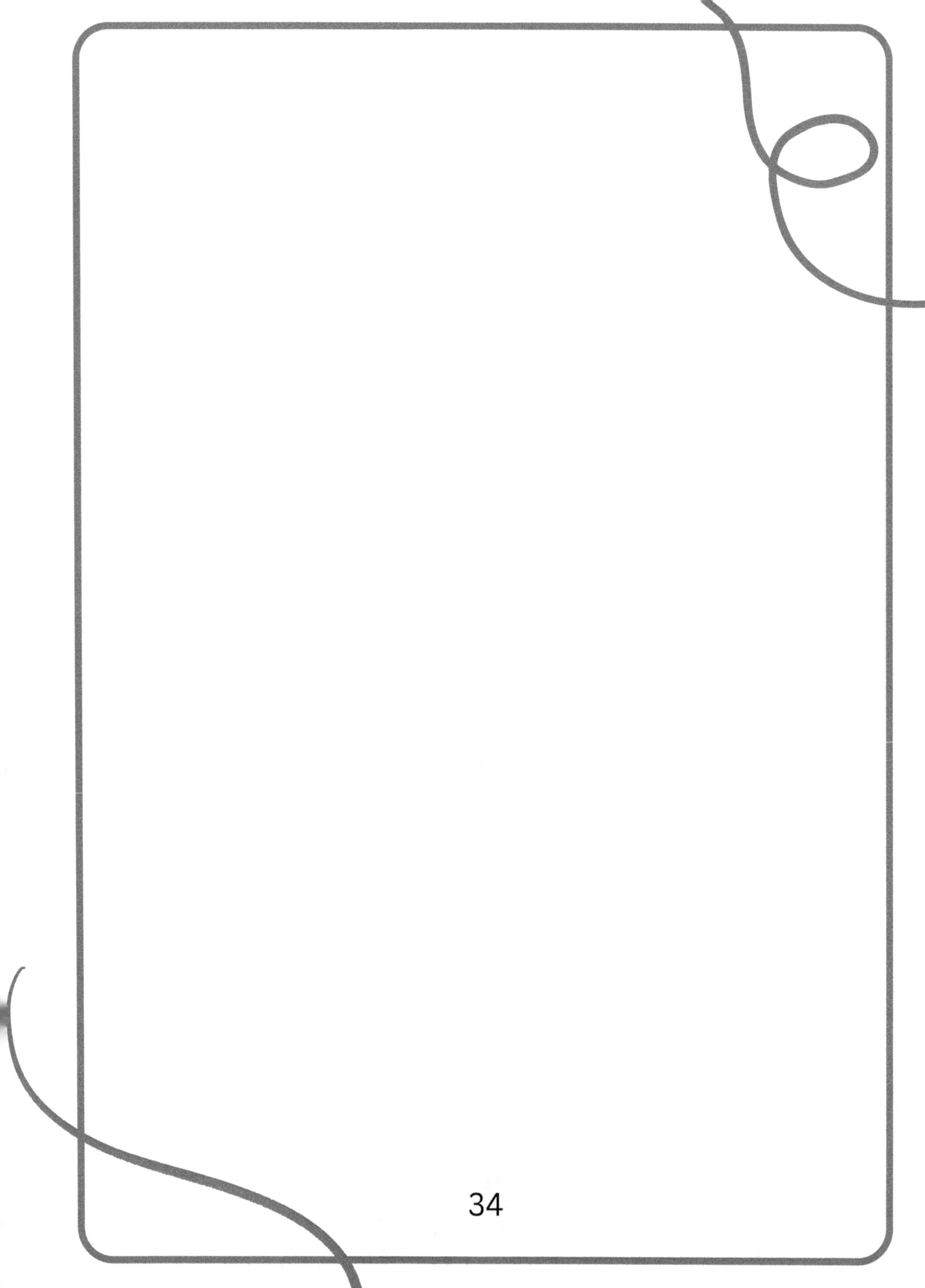

34

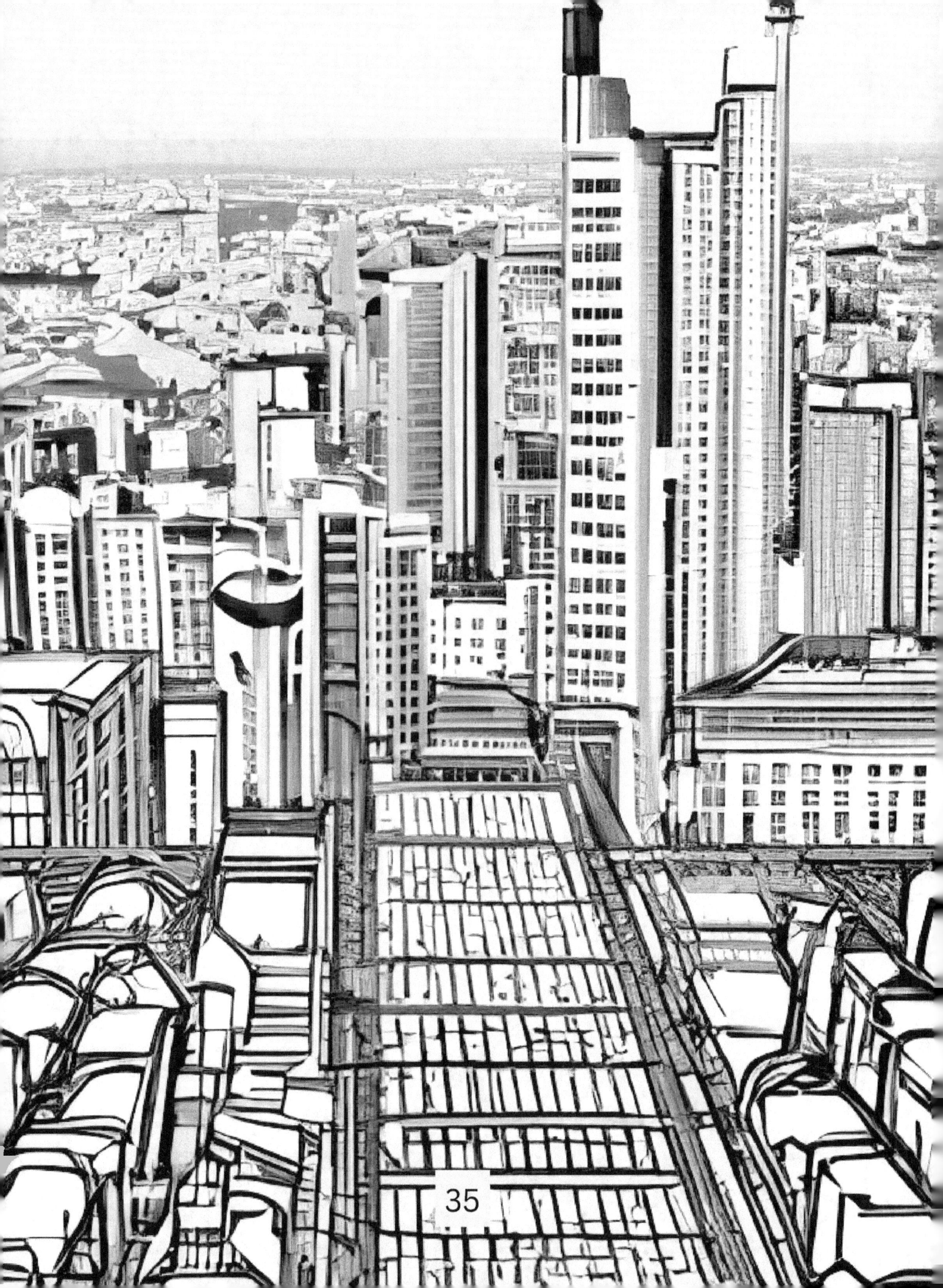

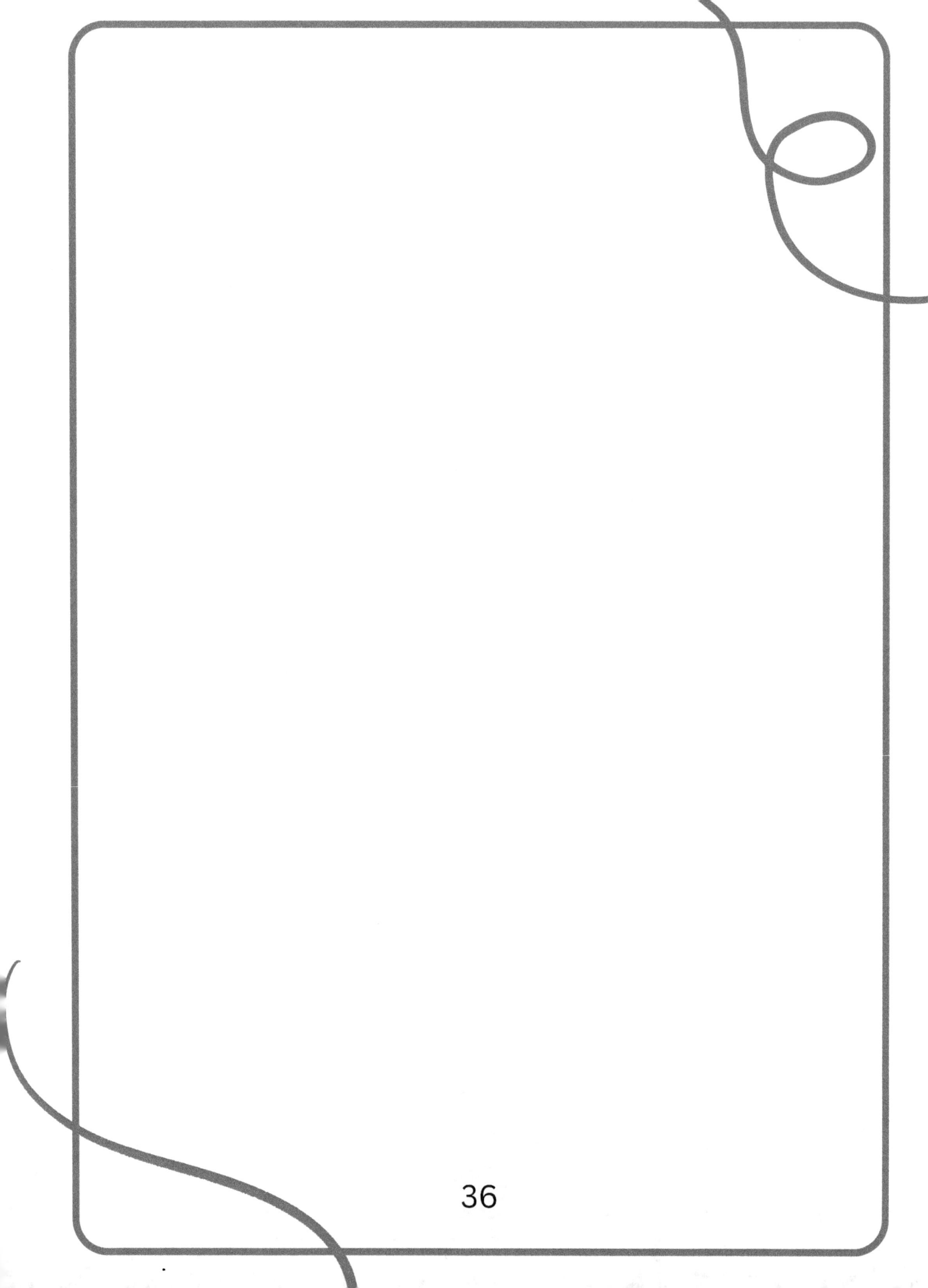

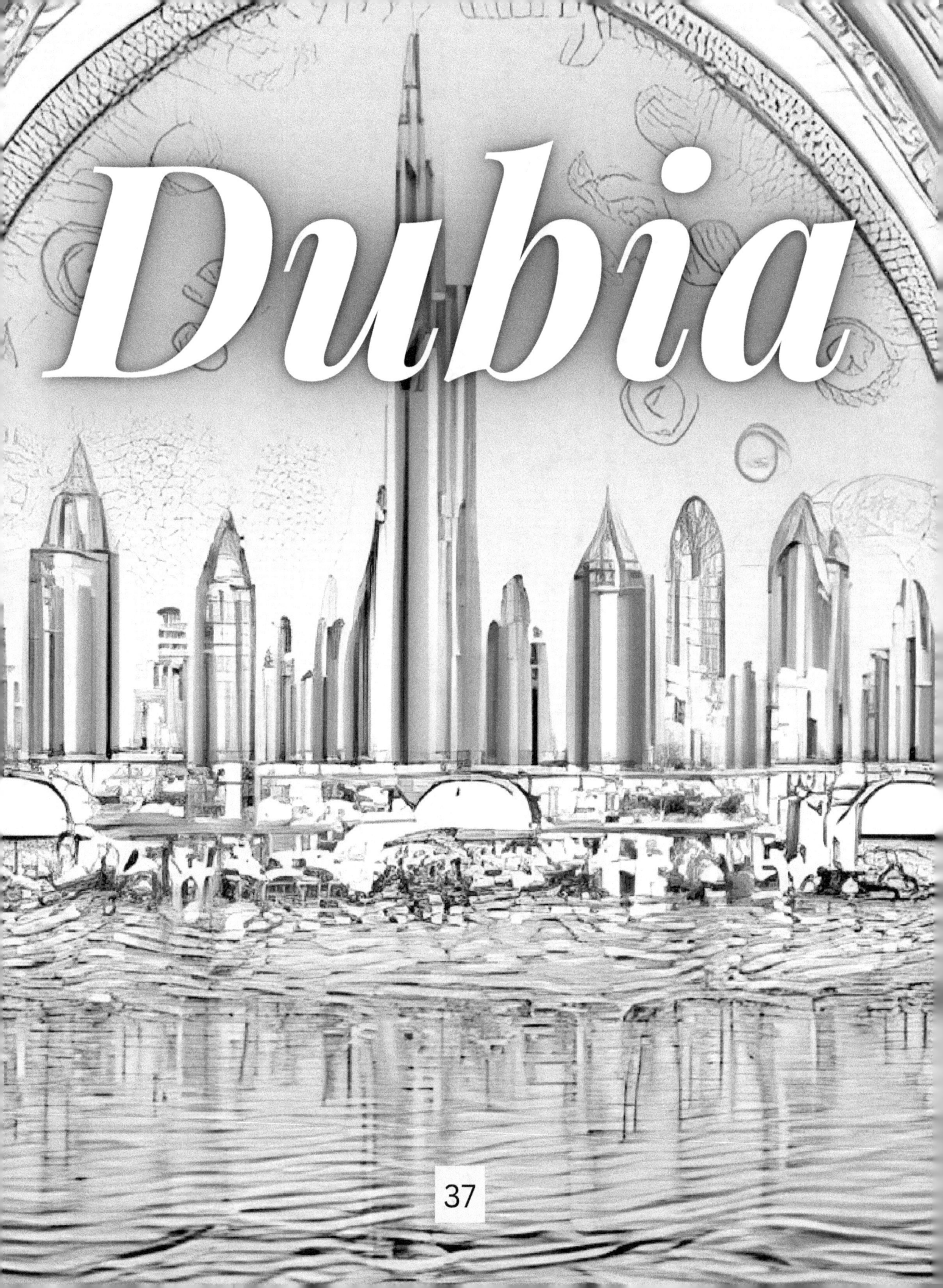

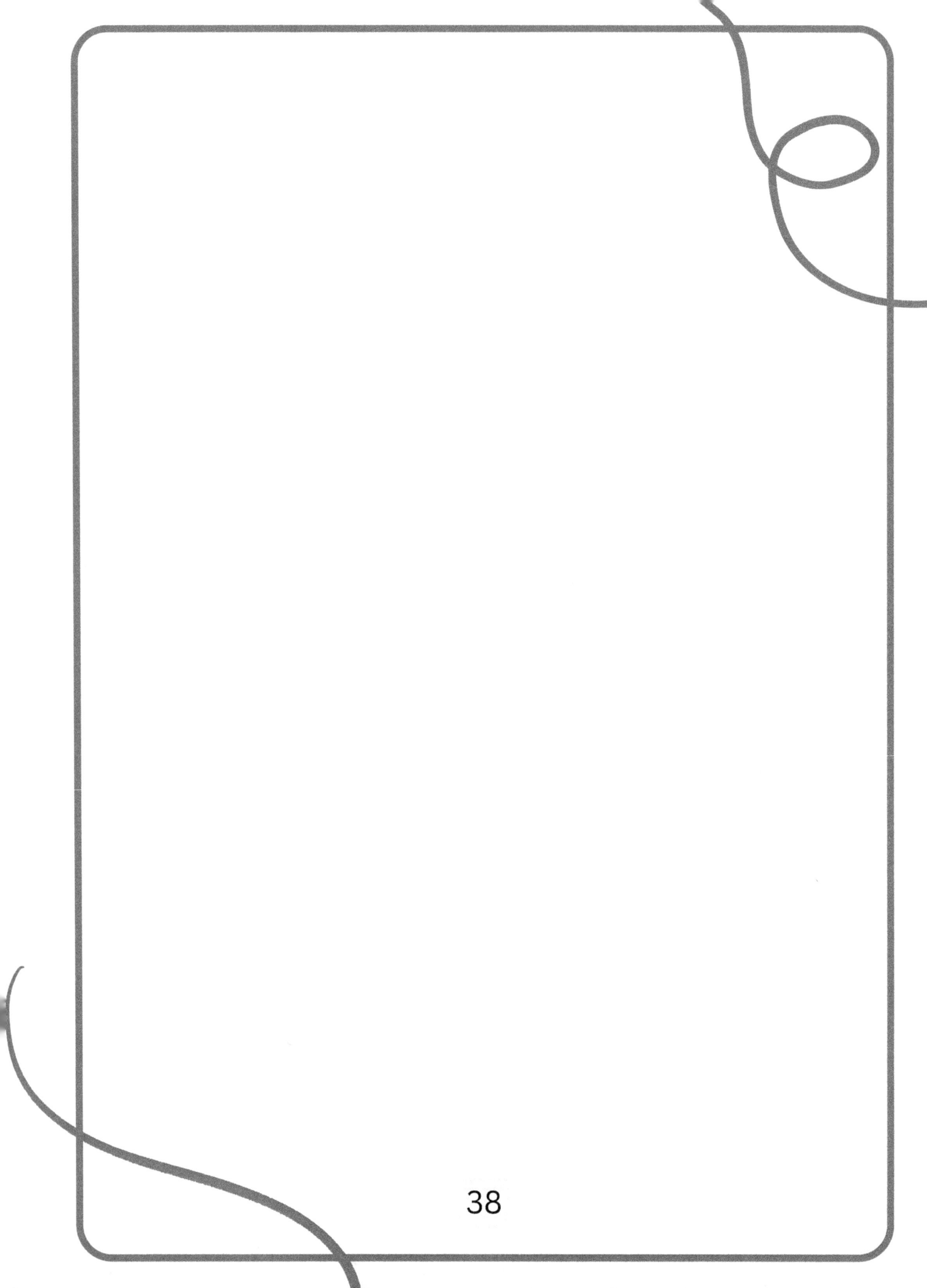

38

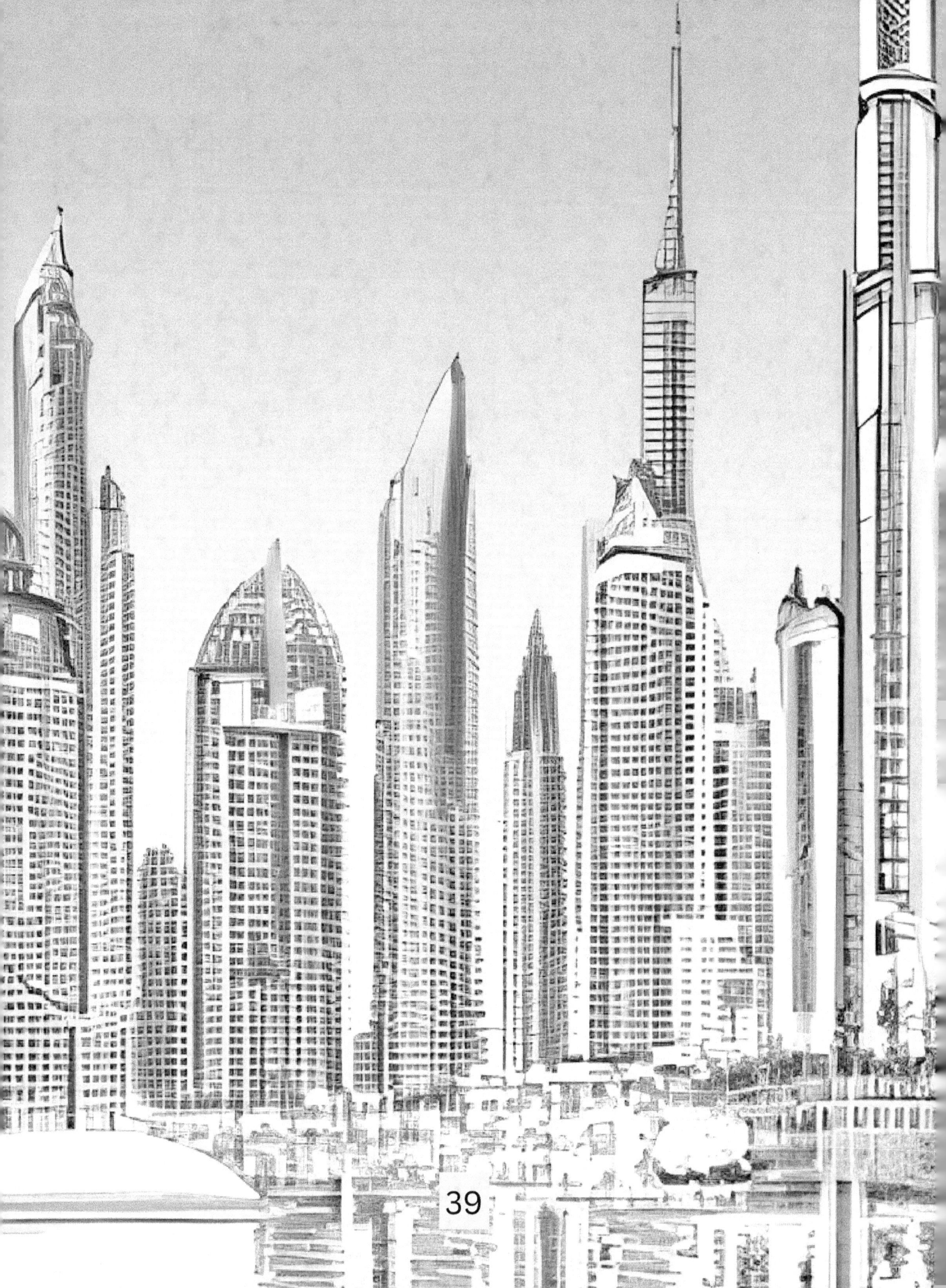

39

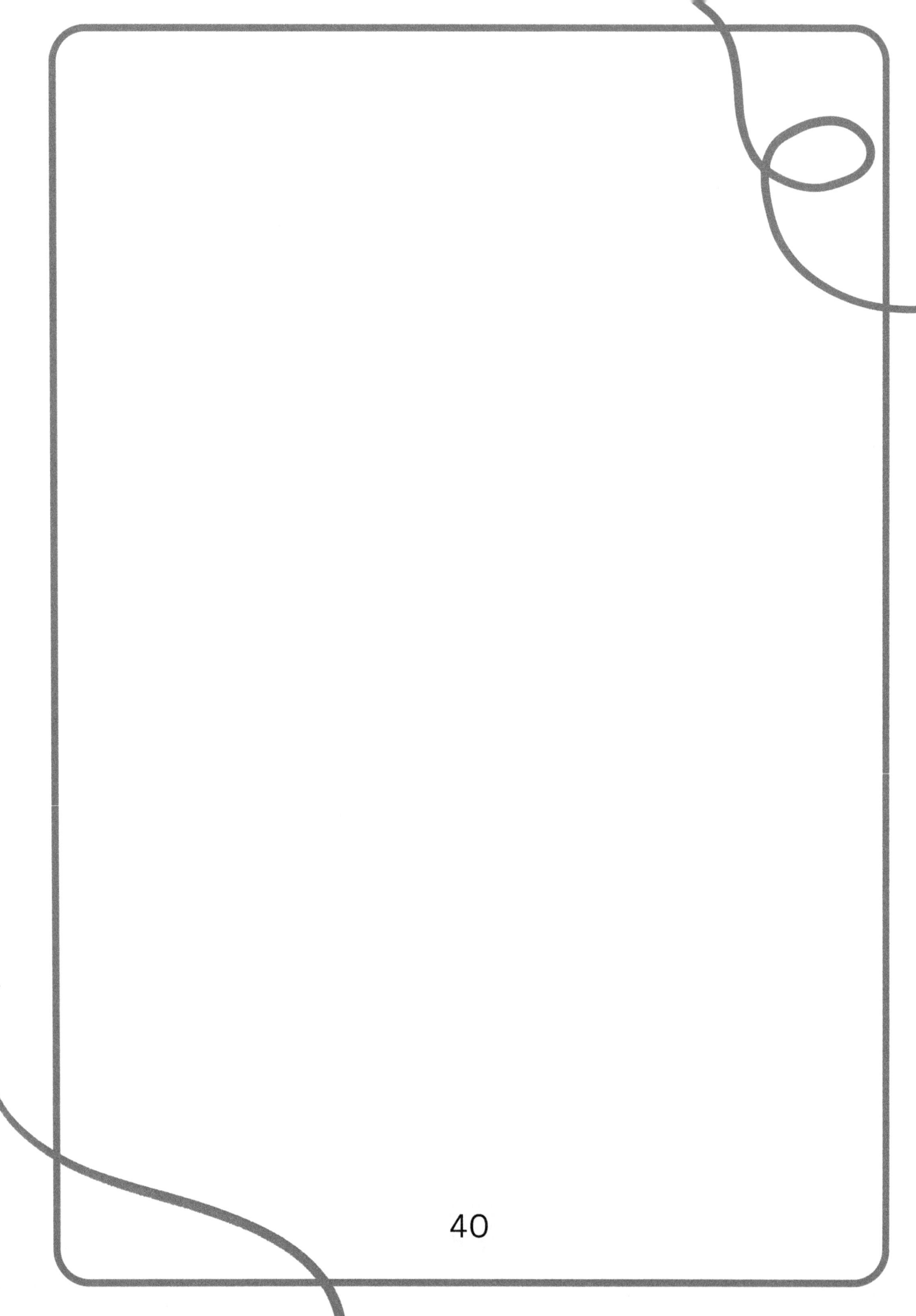

HONG KONG

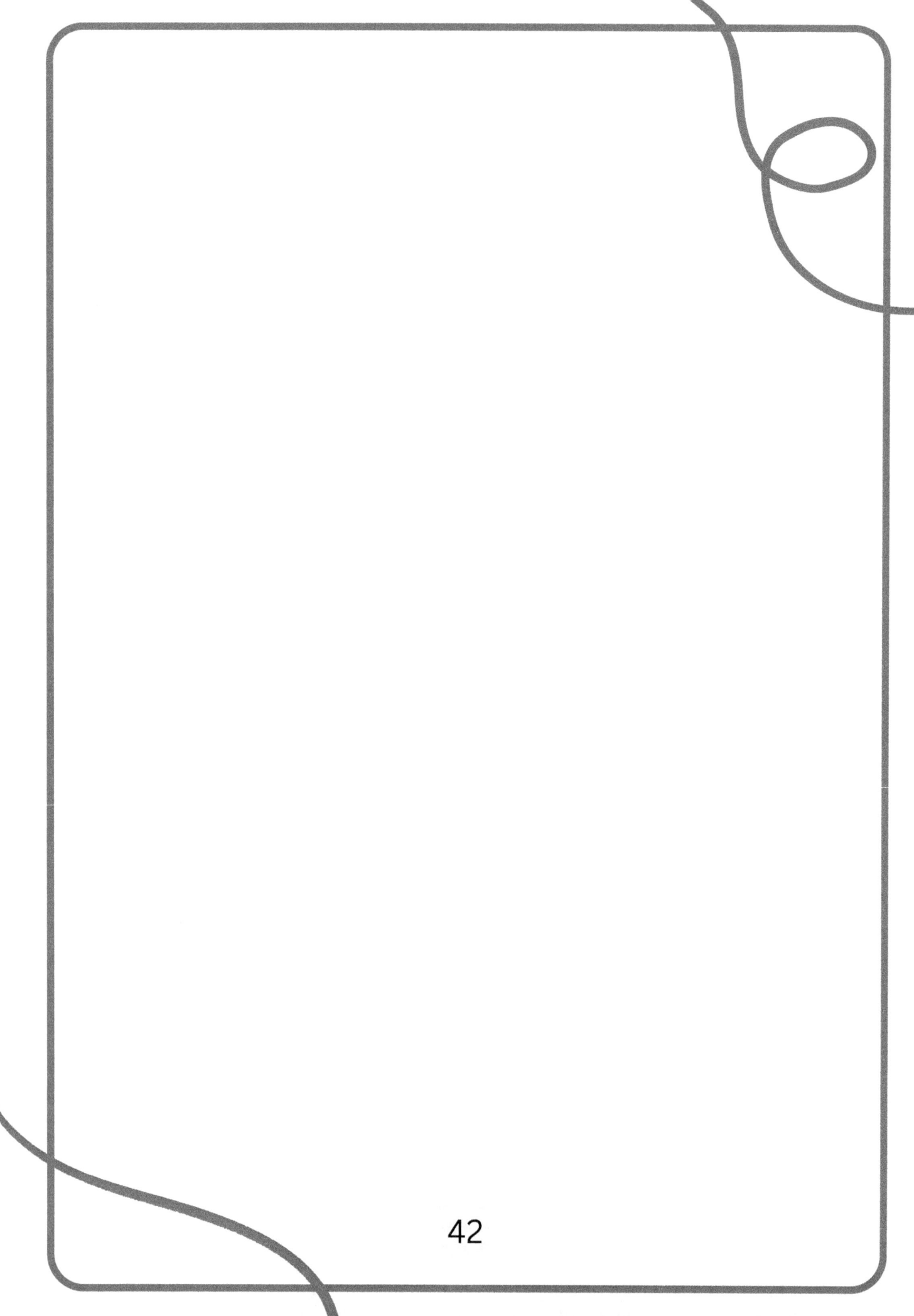

42

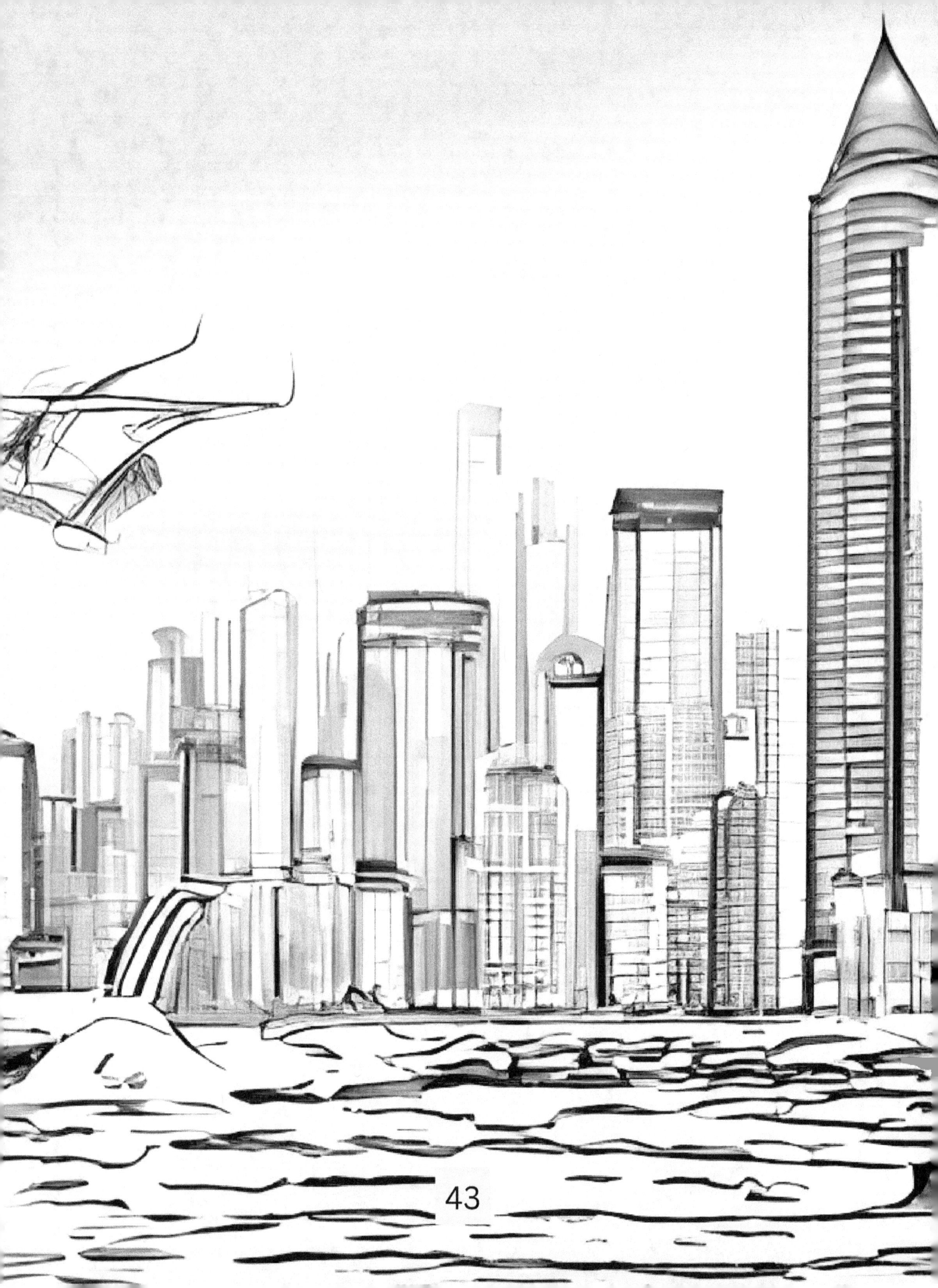

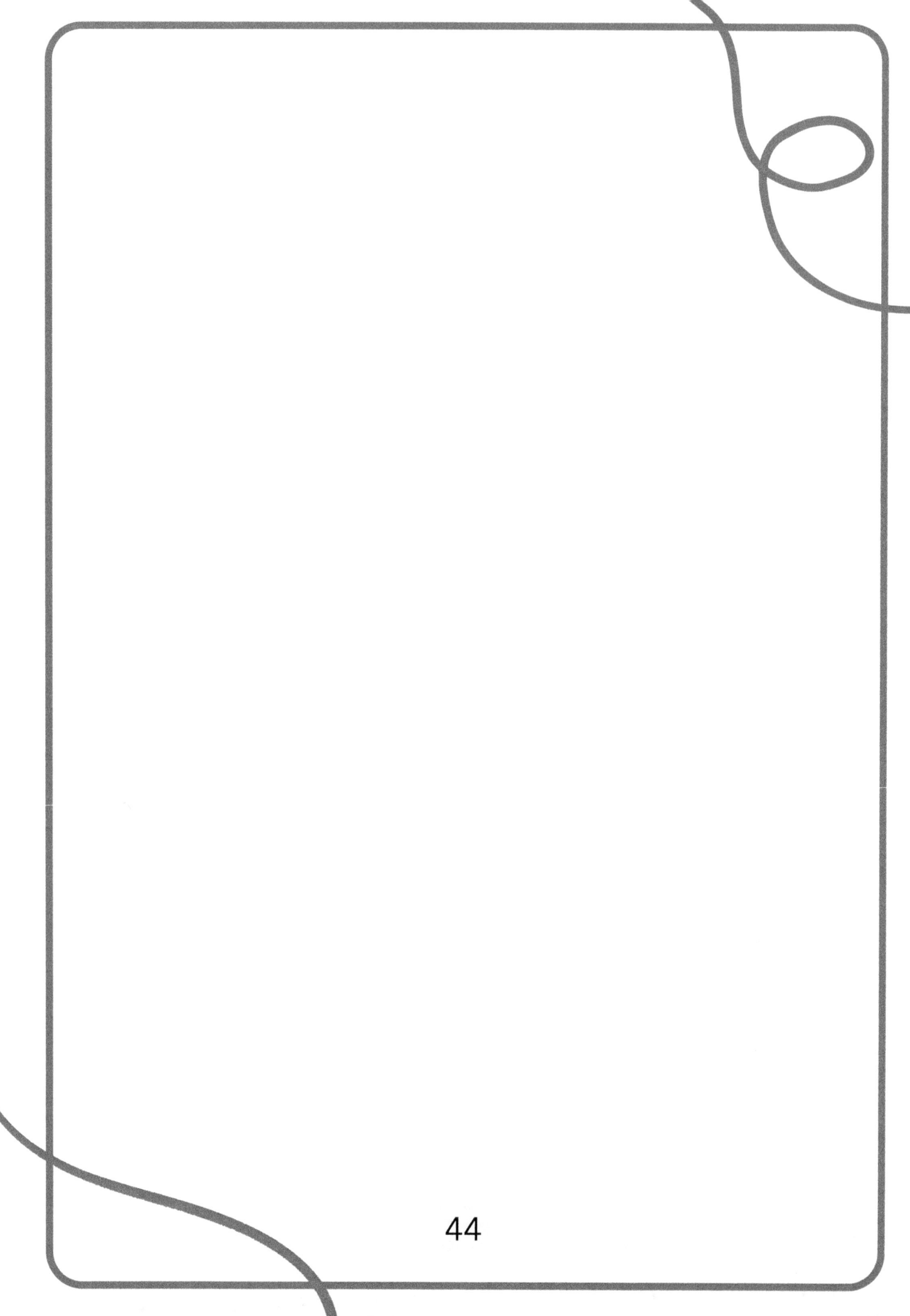

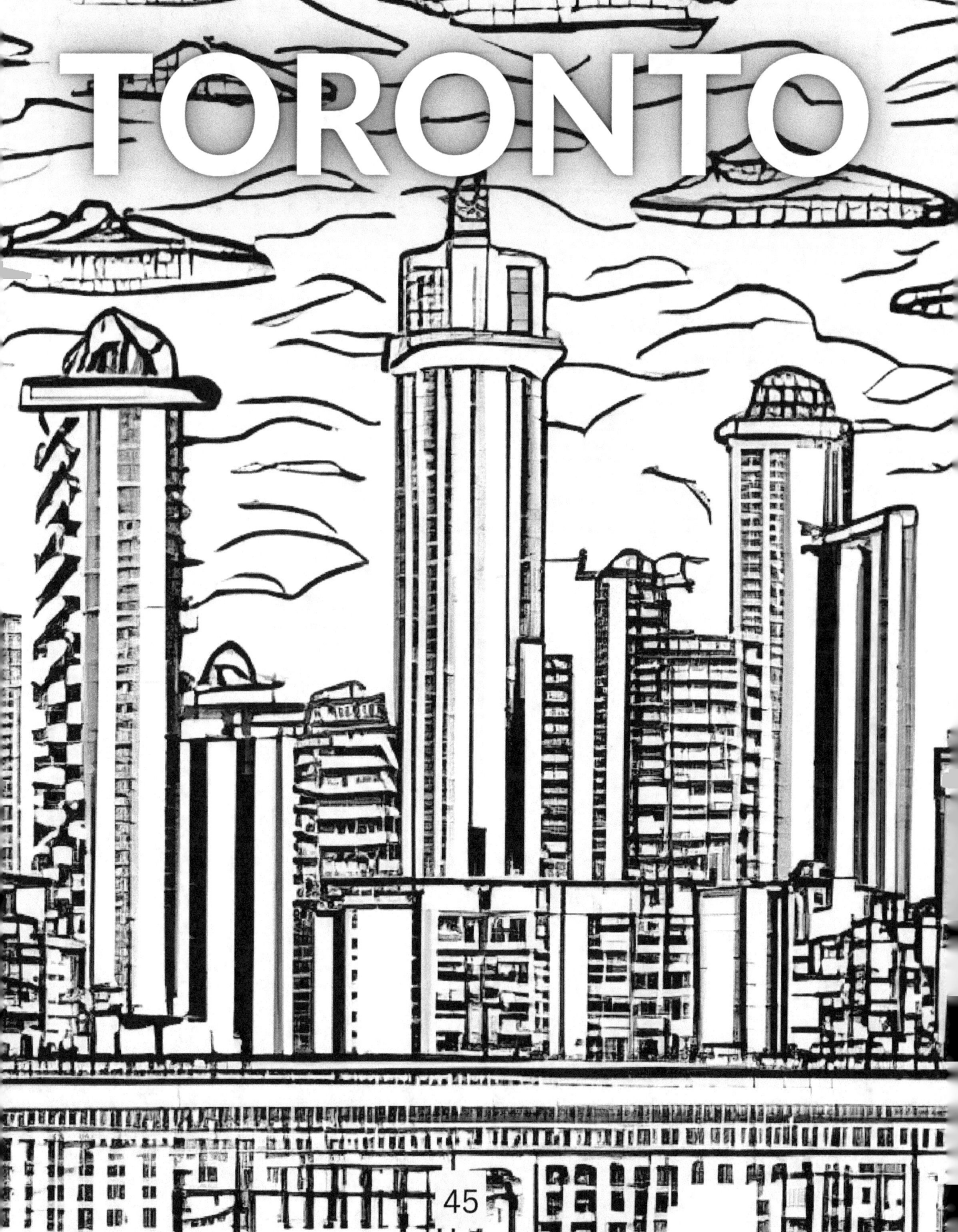

TORONTO

45

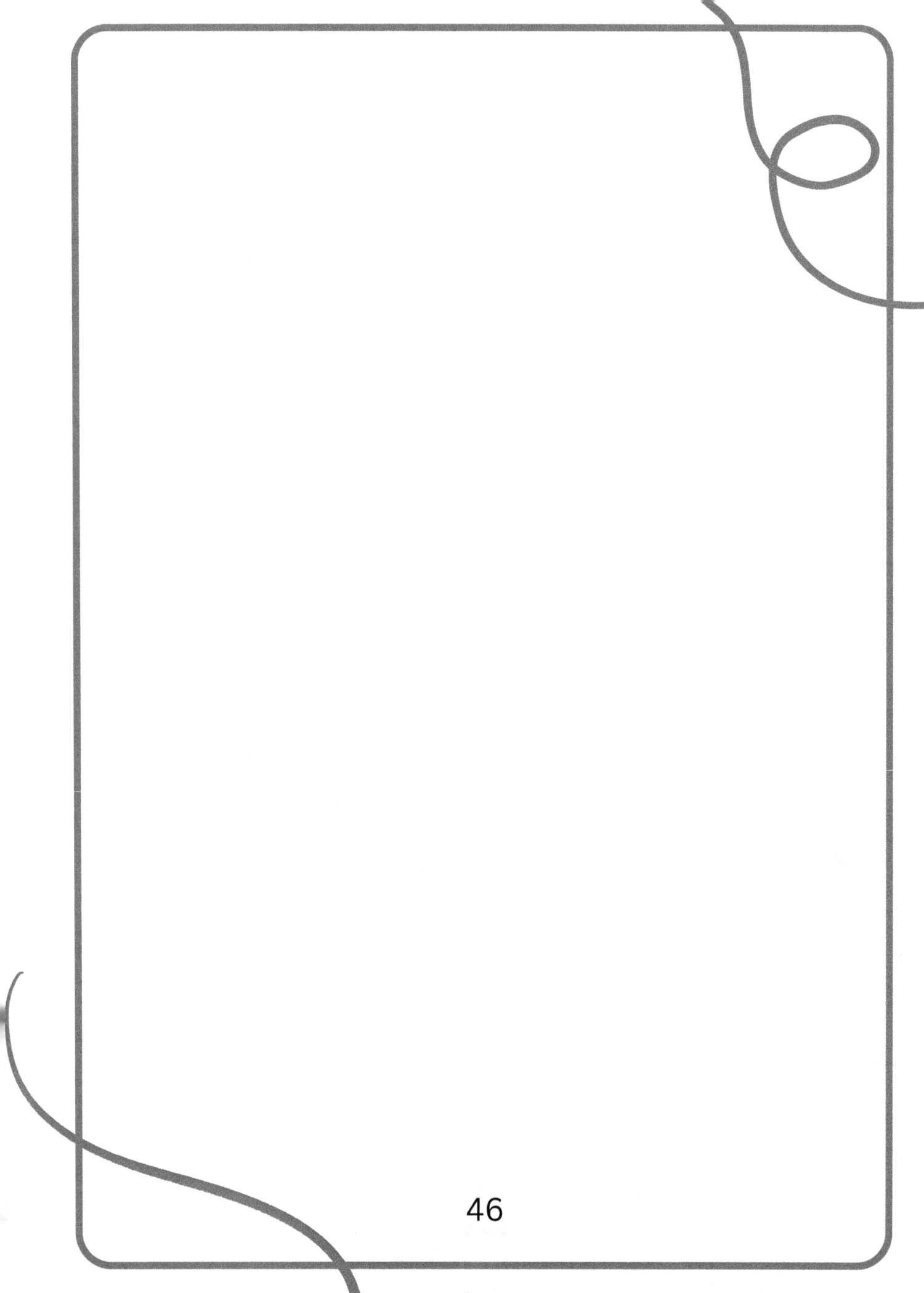

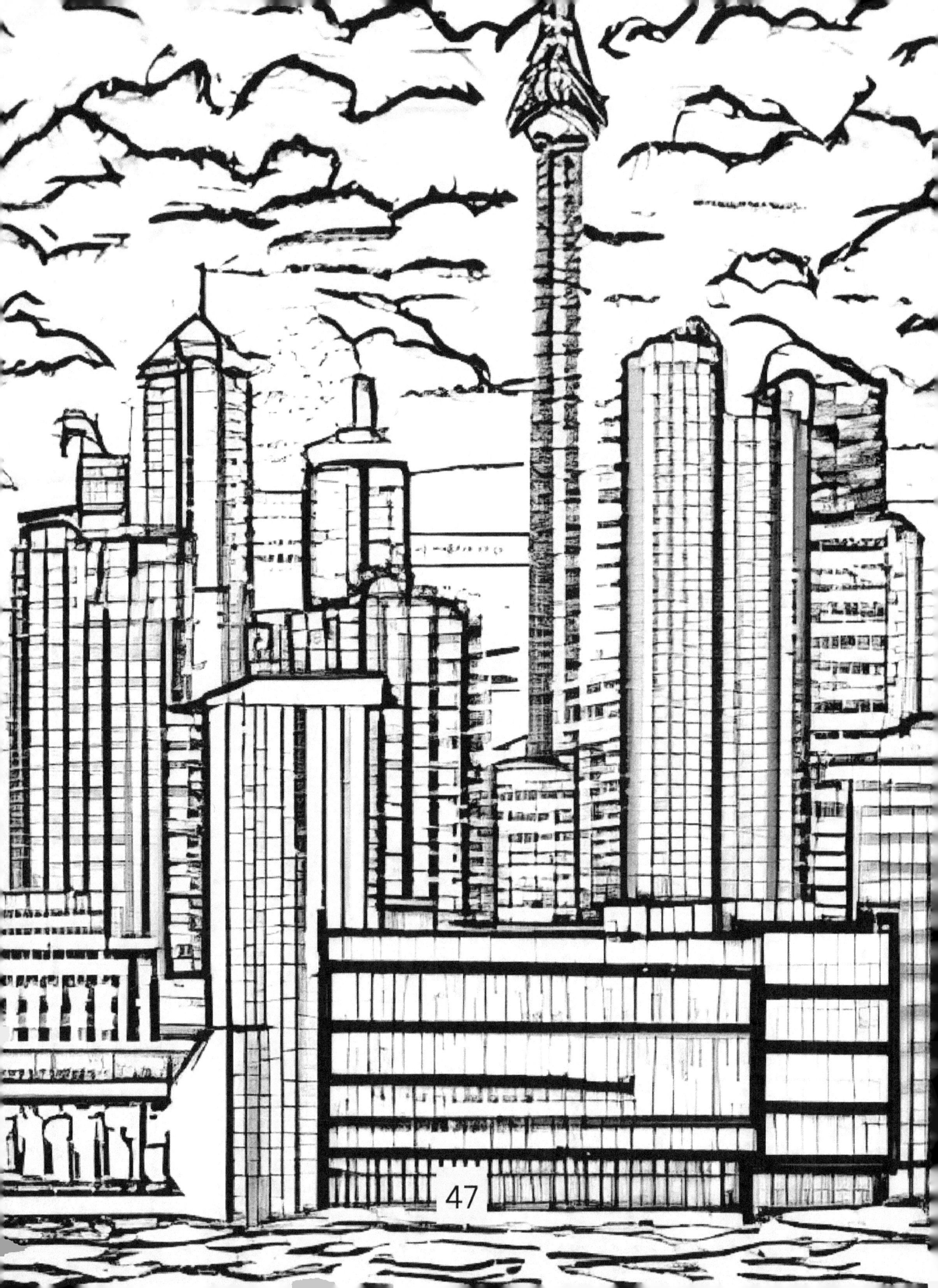

47

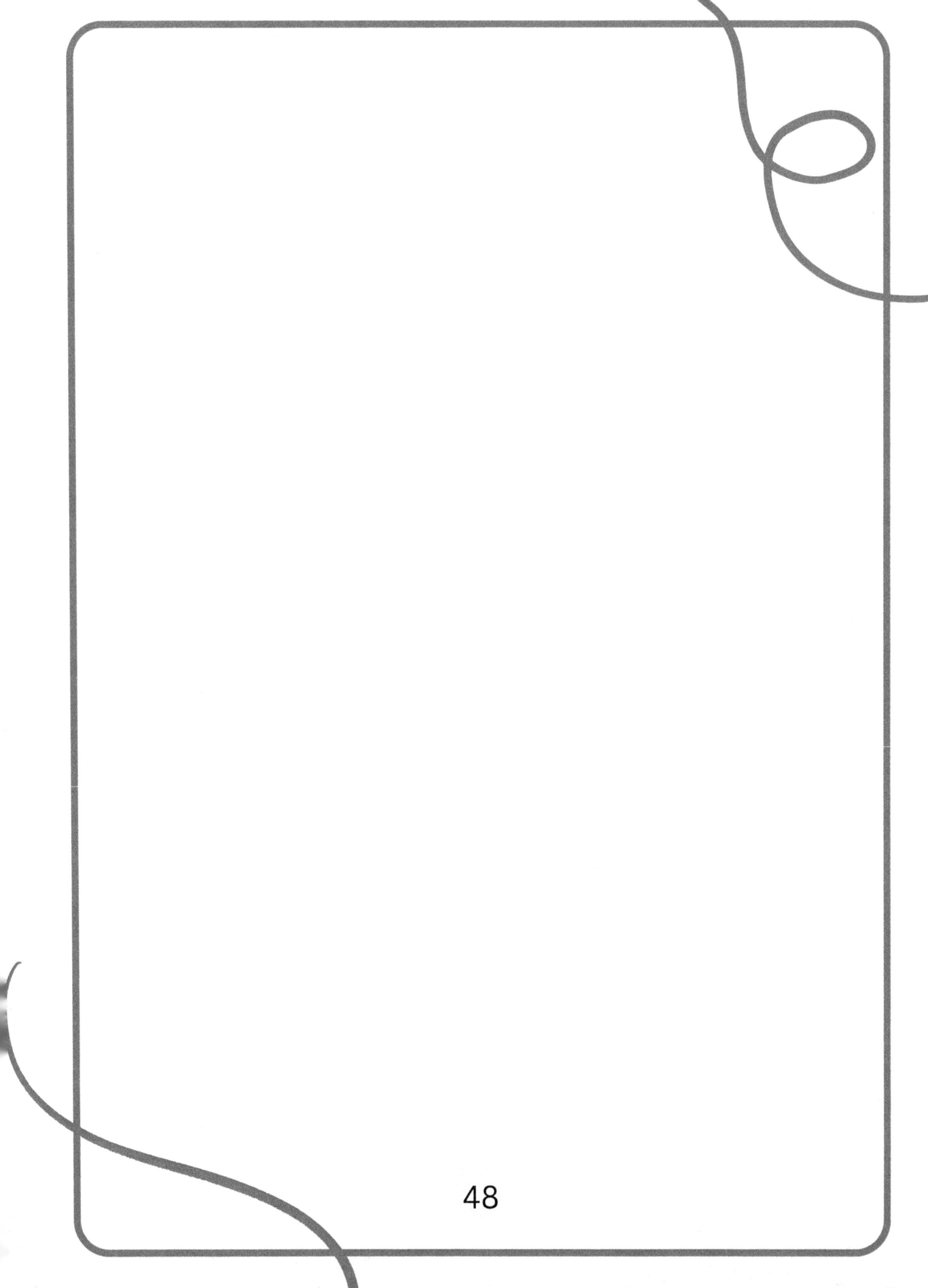

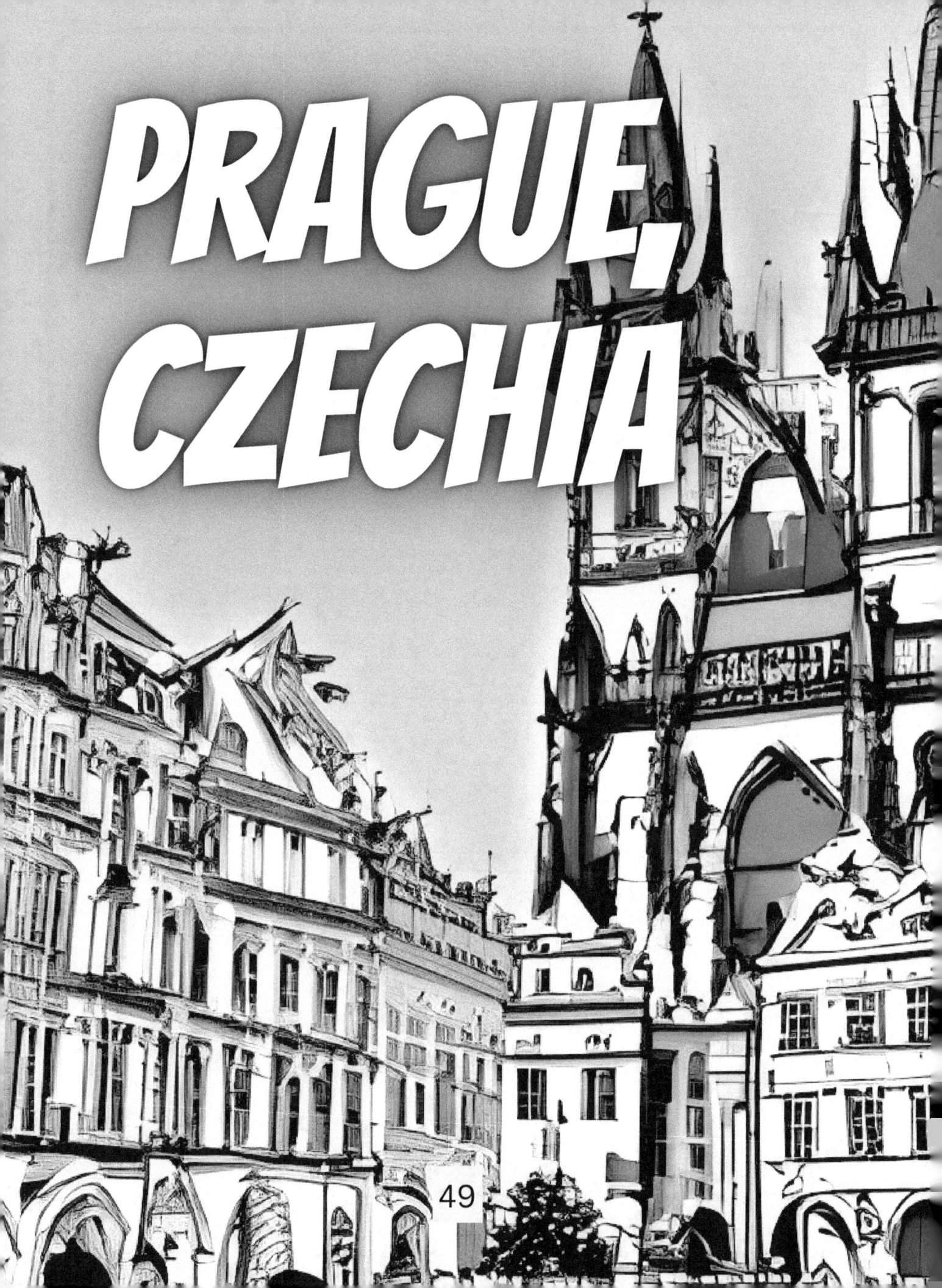

PRAGUE, CZECHIA

49

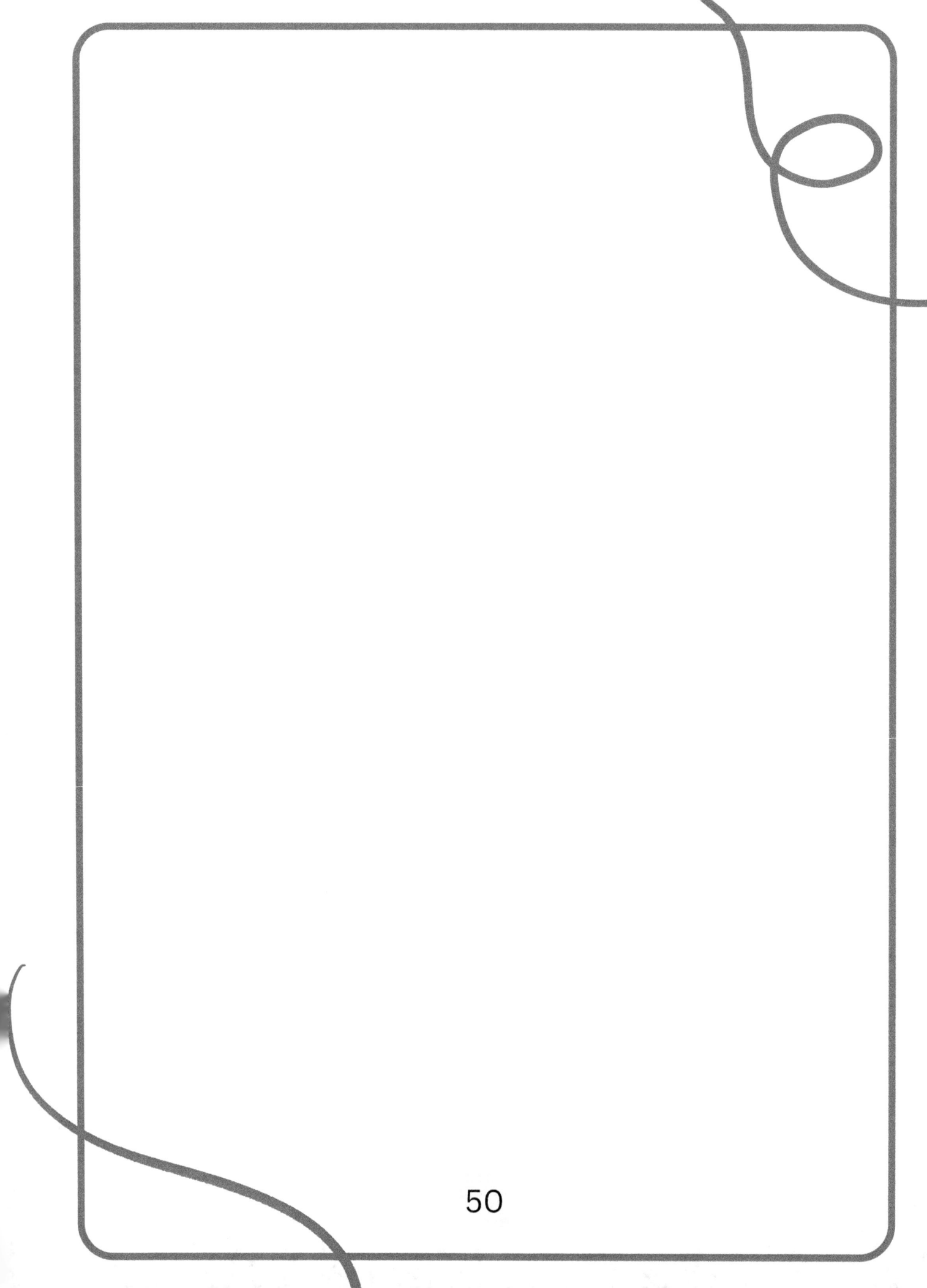

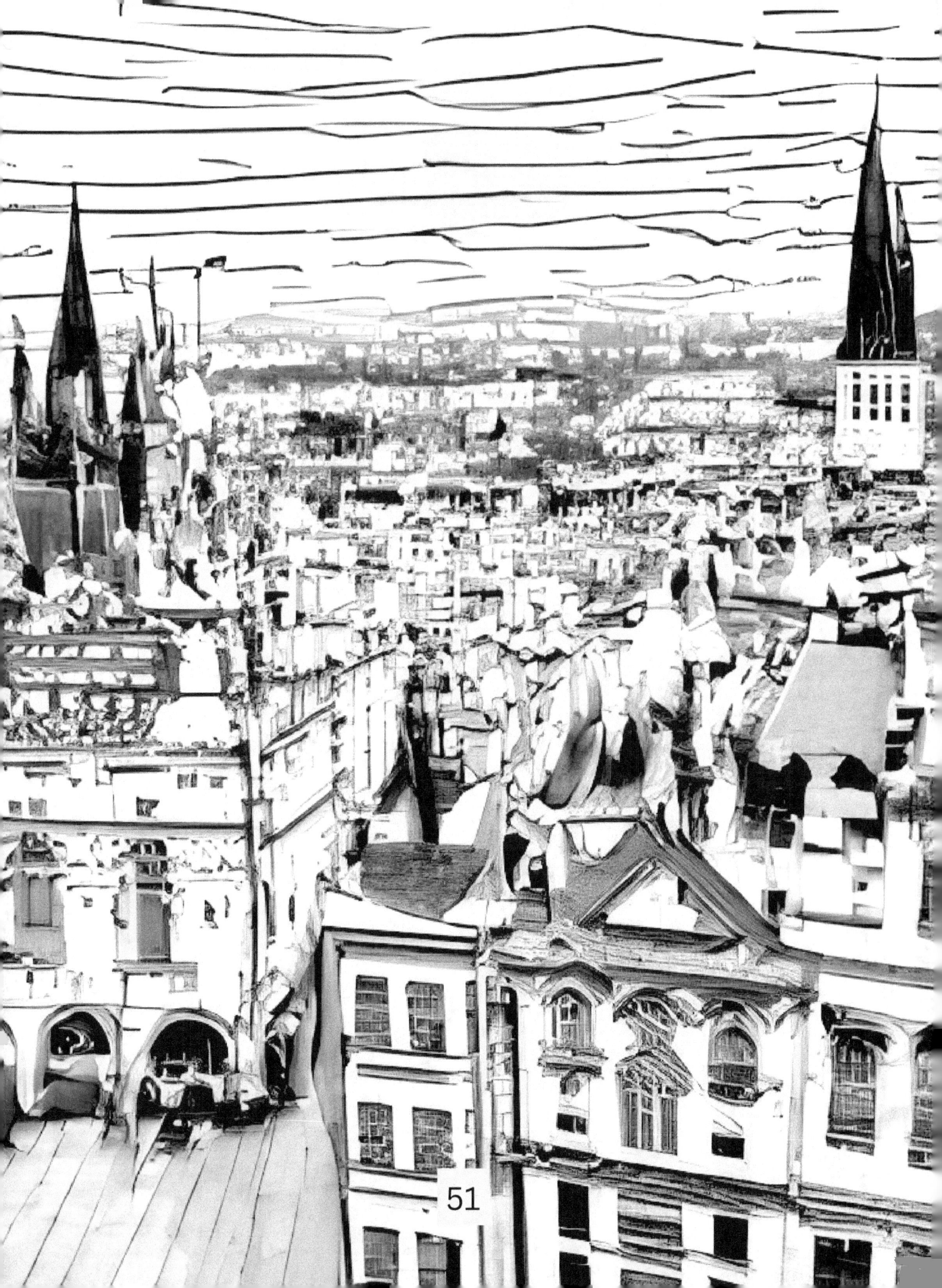

51

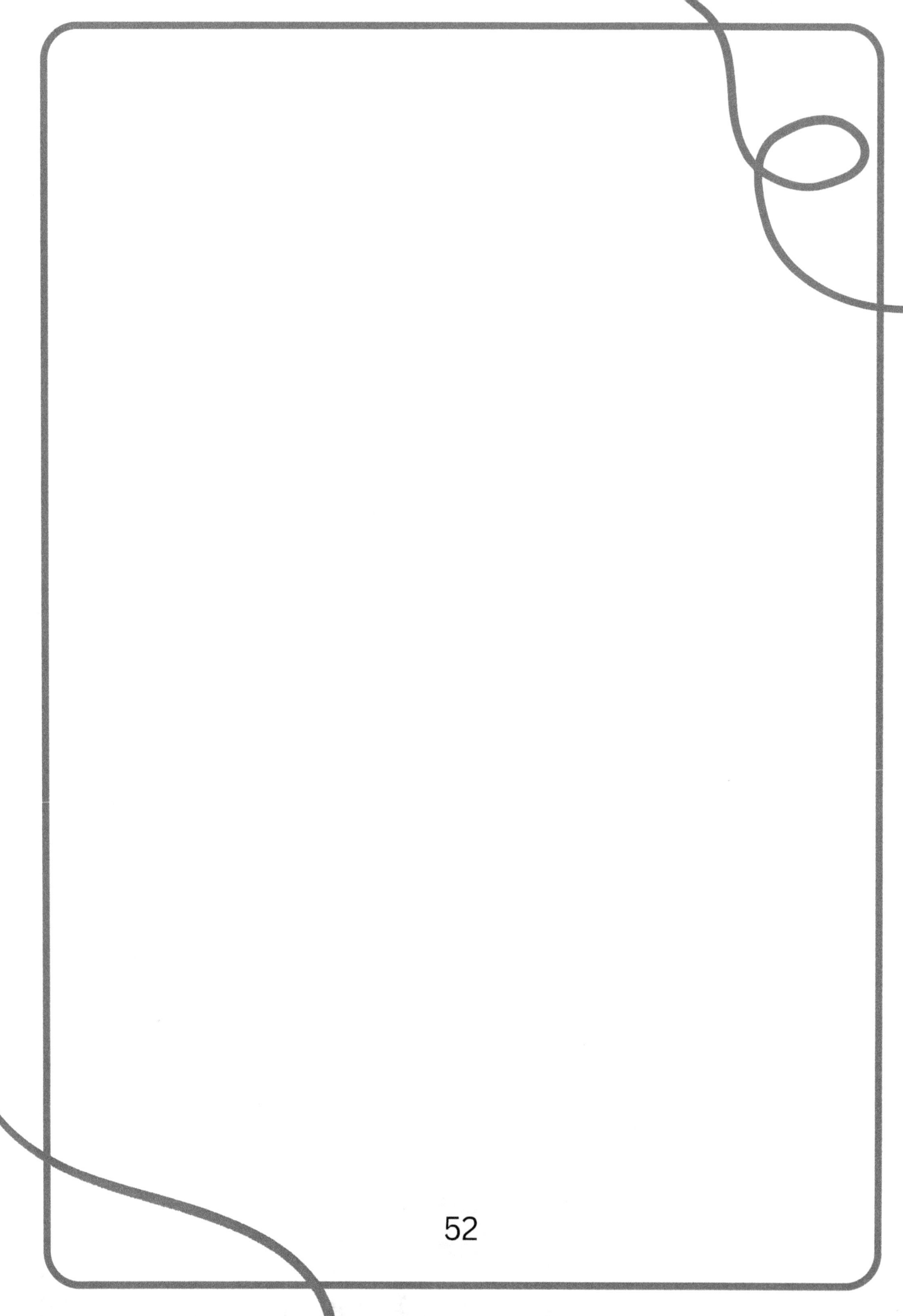

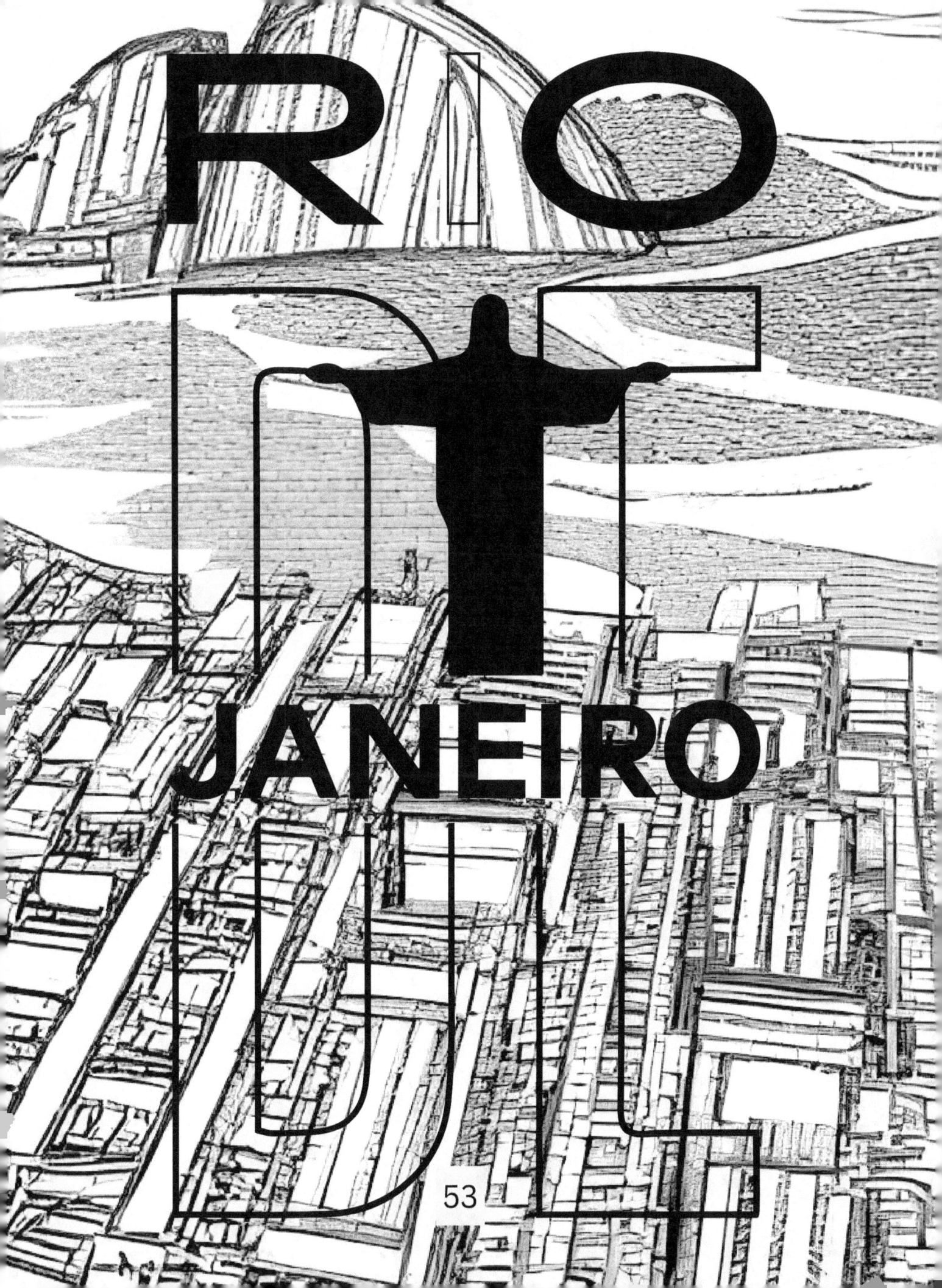

RIO DE JANEIRO

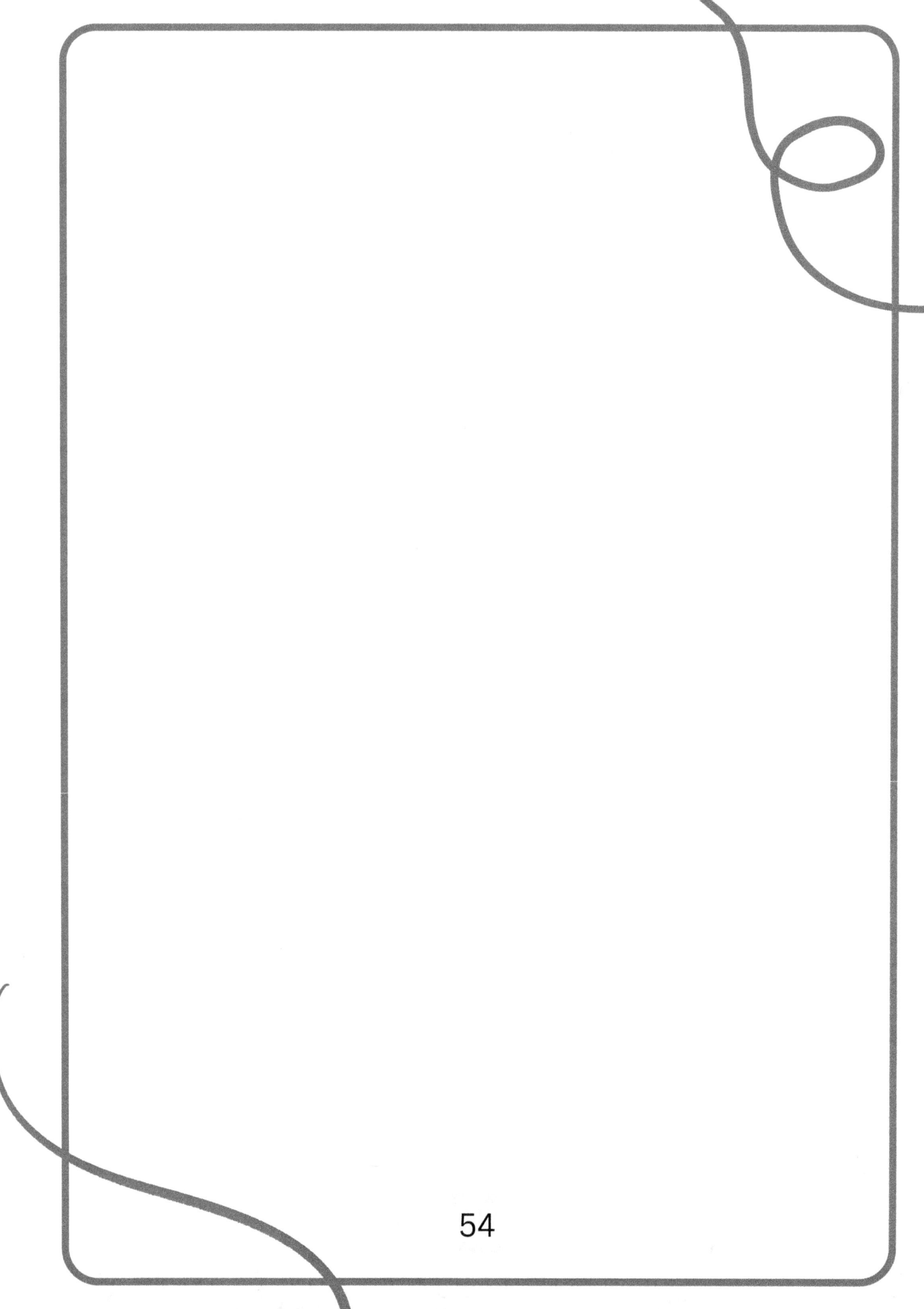

54

55

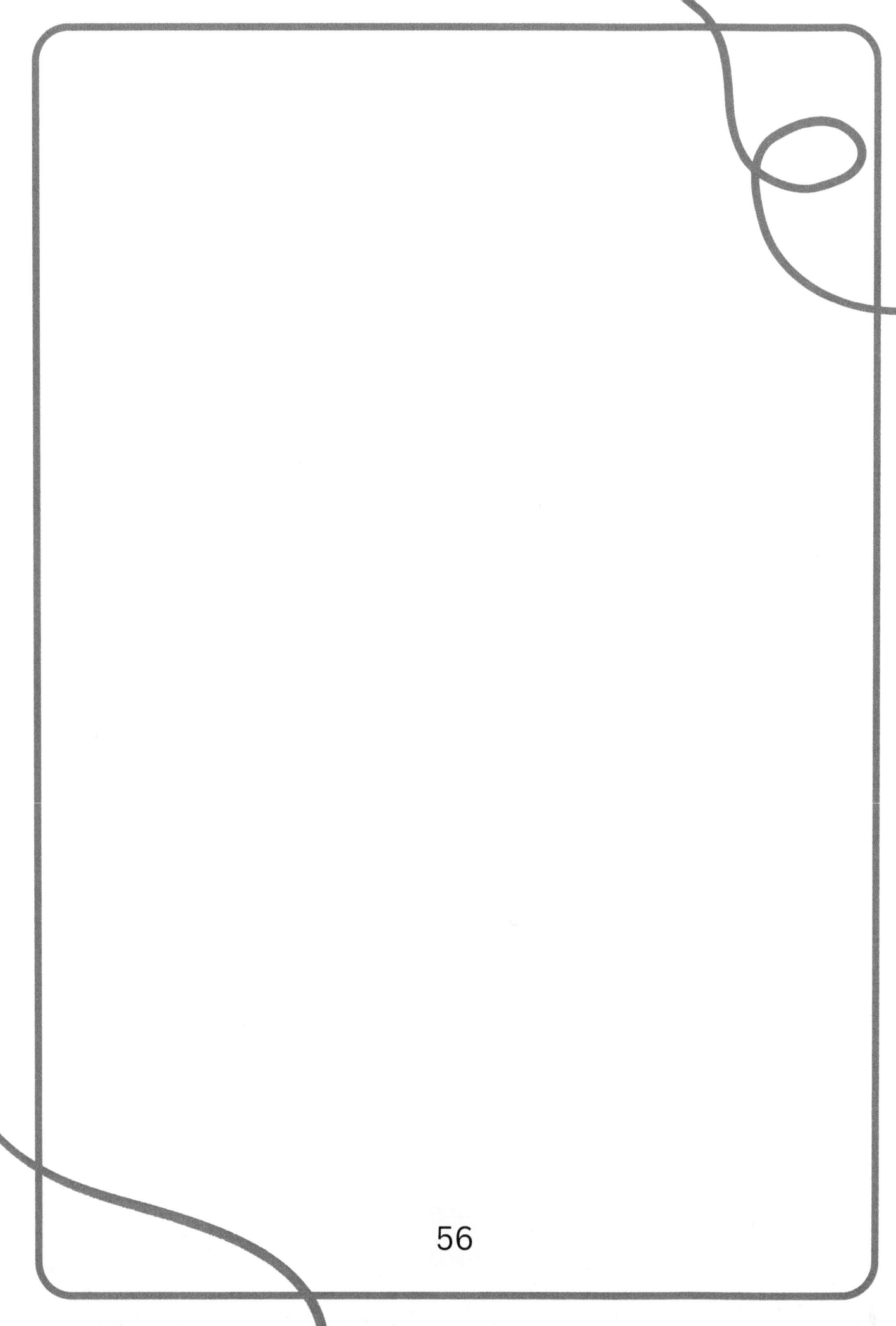

Panama City, Panama

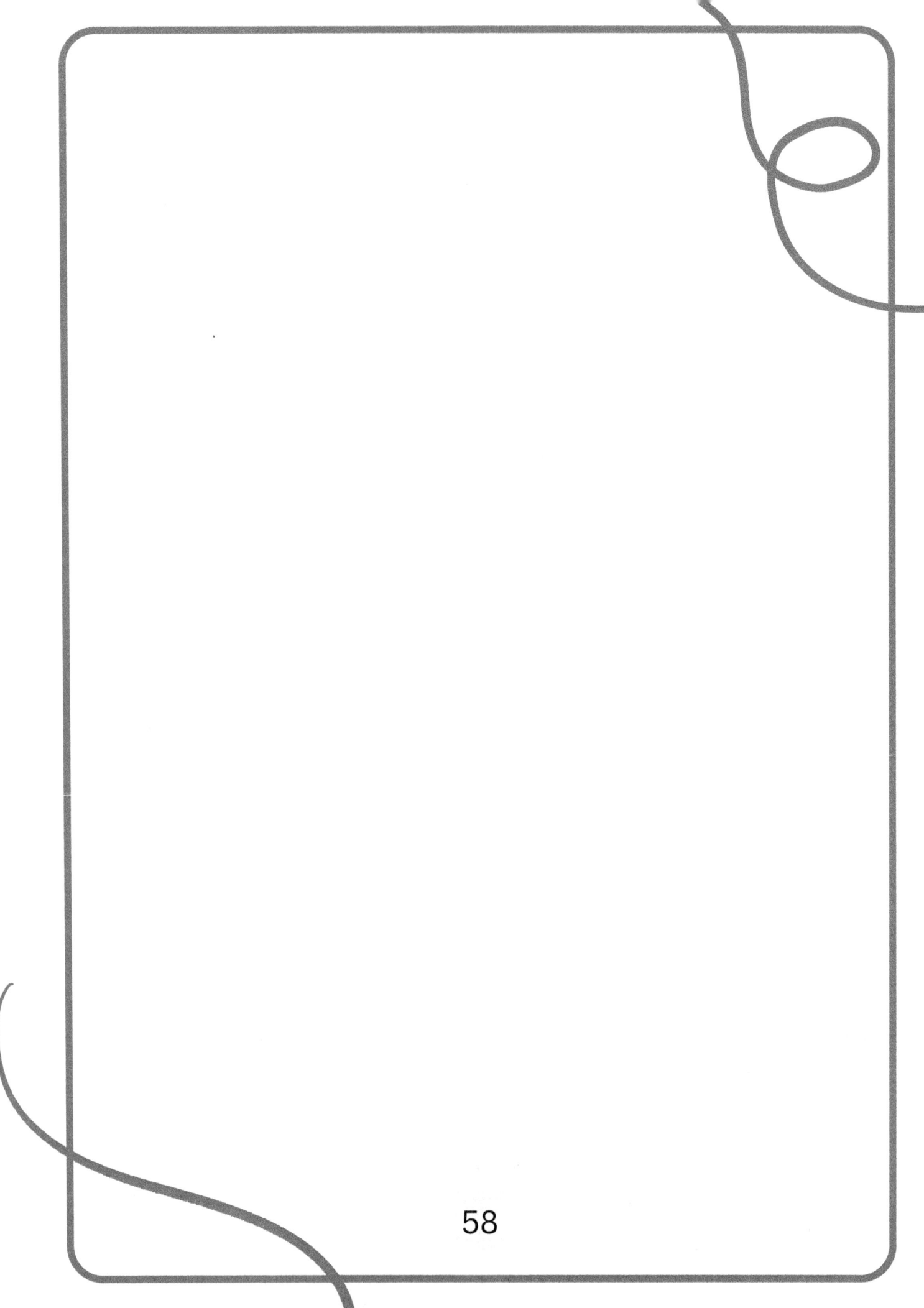

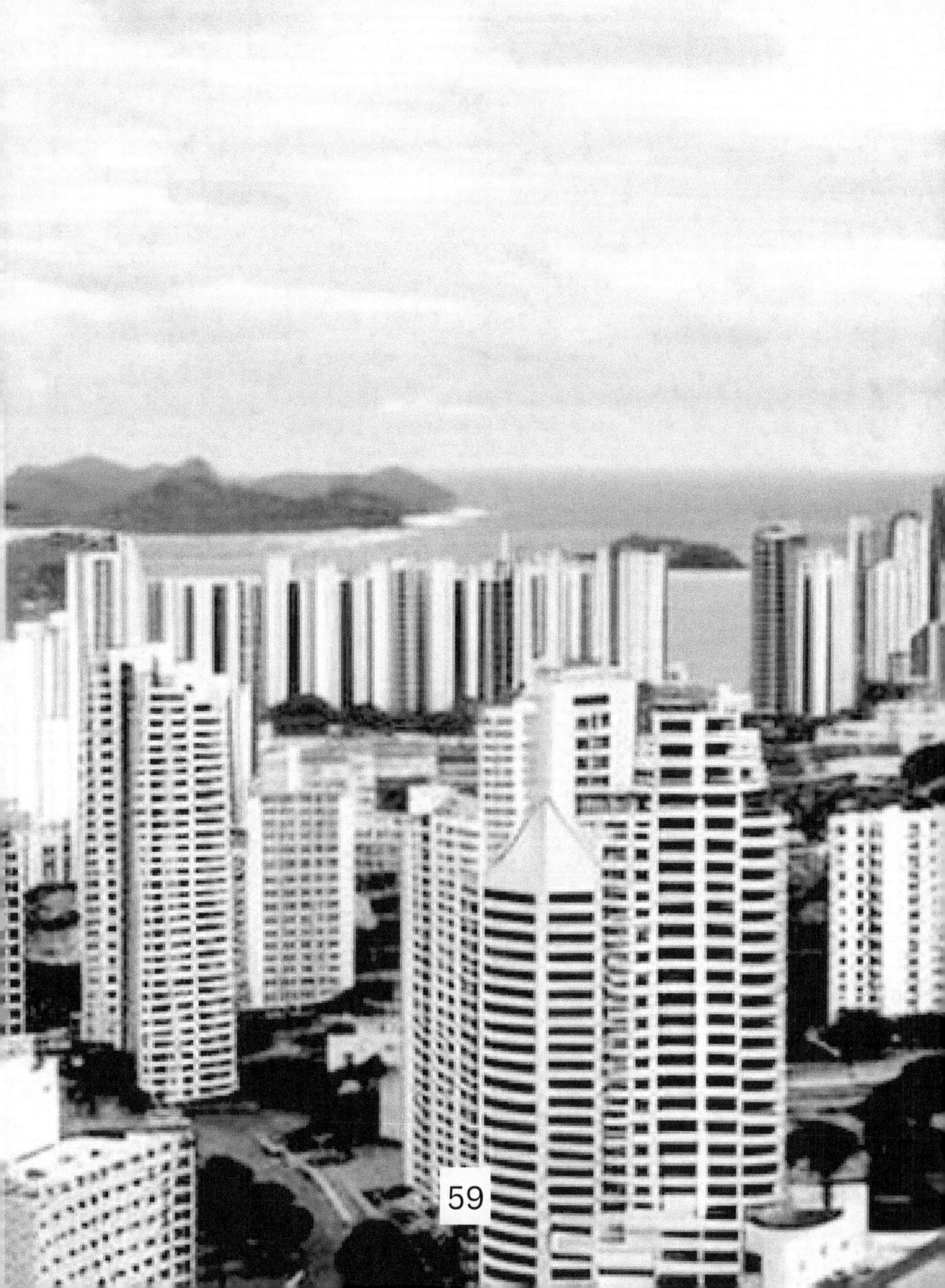

59

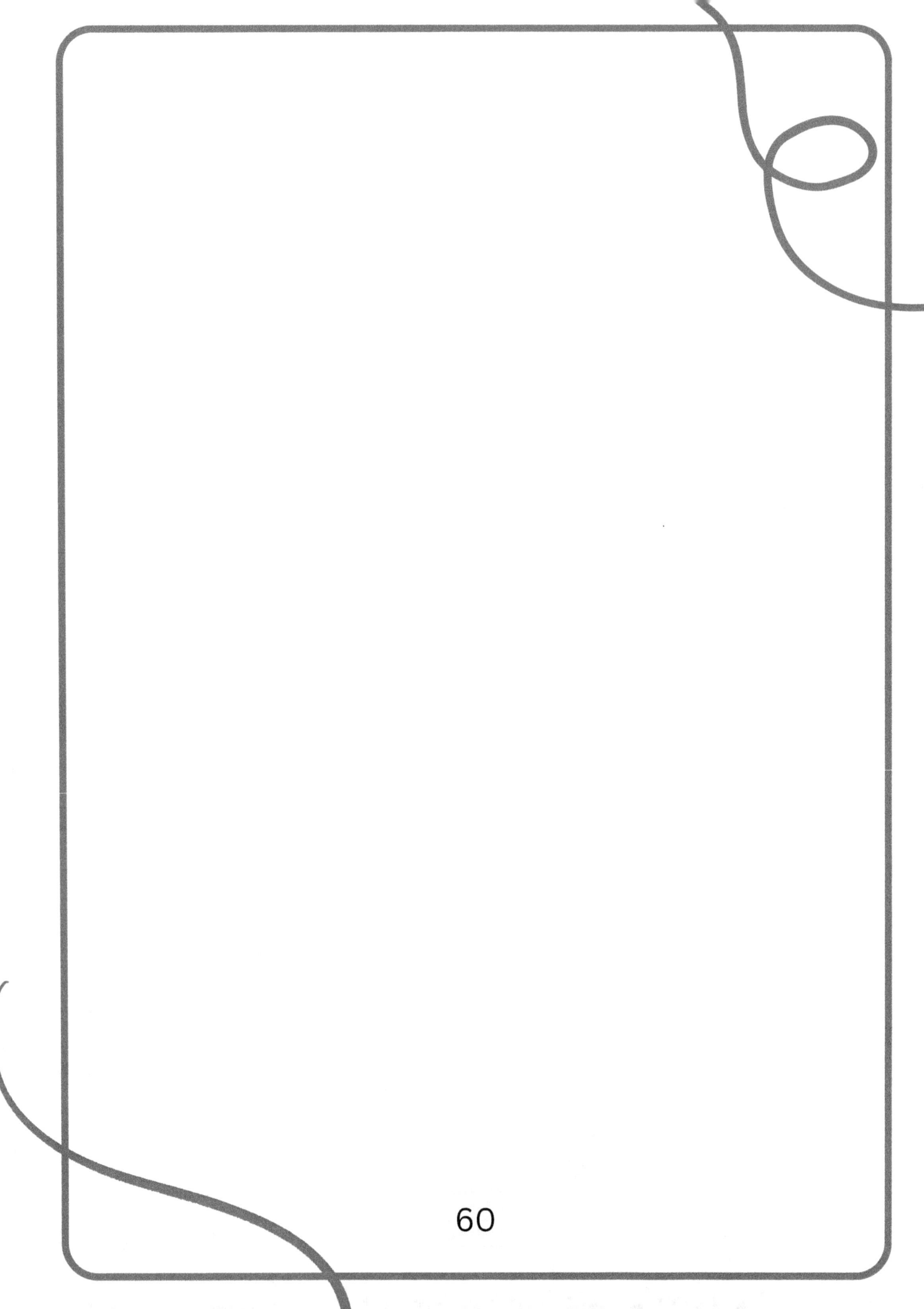

60

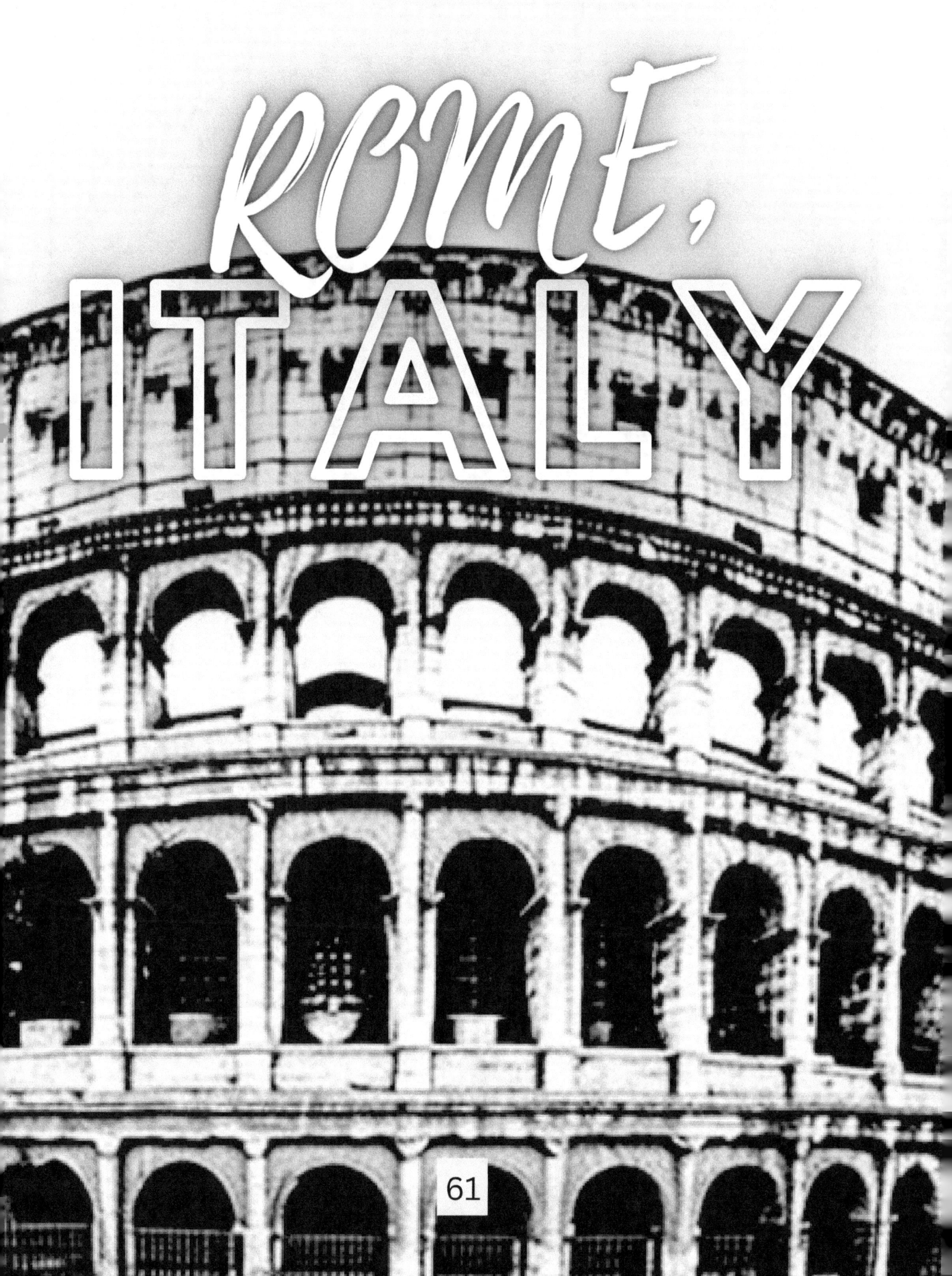

ROME, ITALY

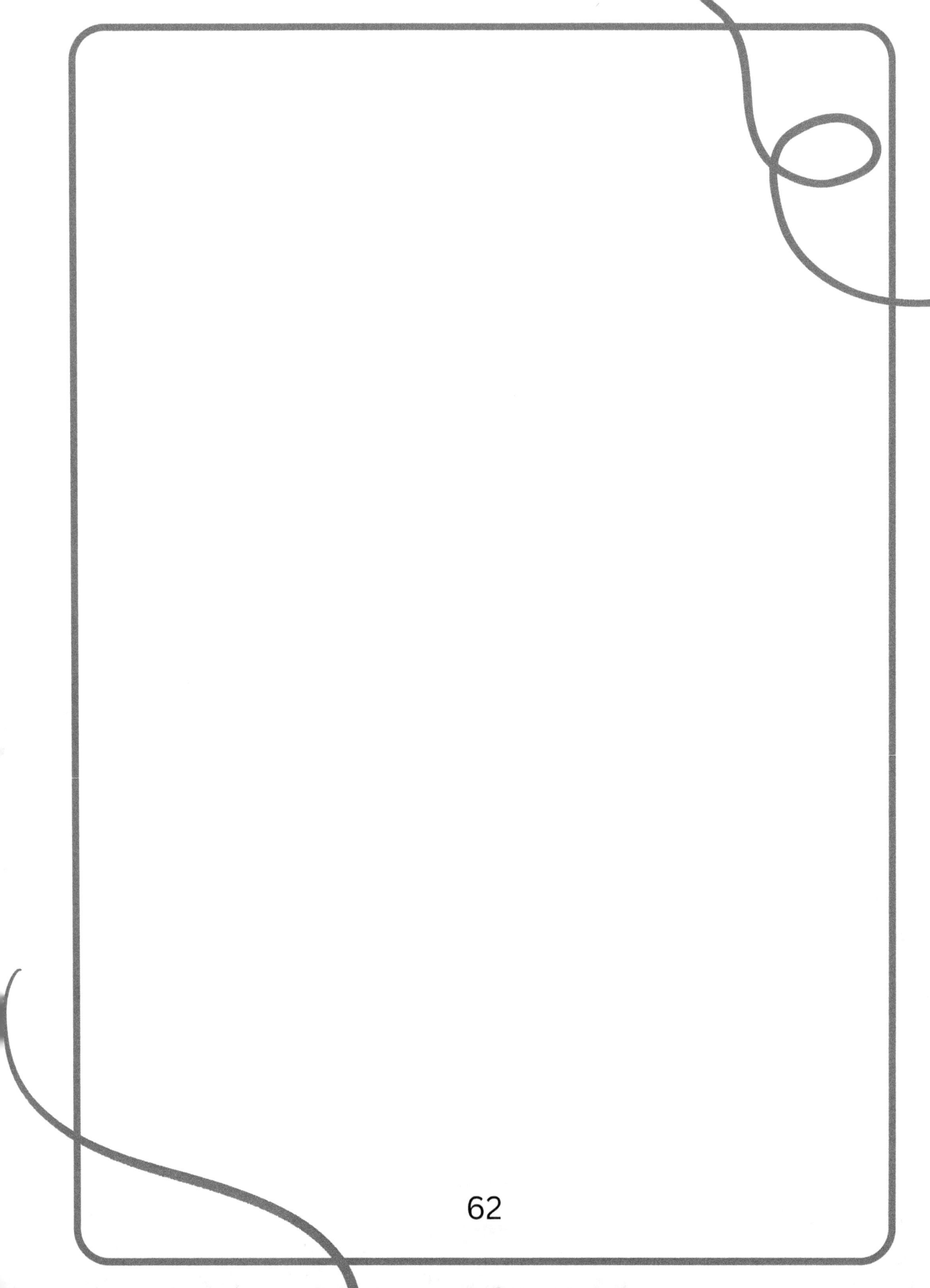

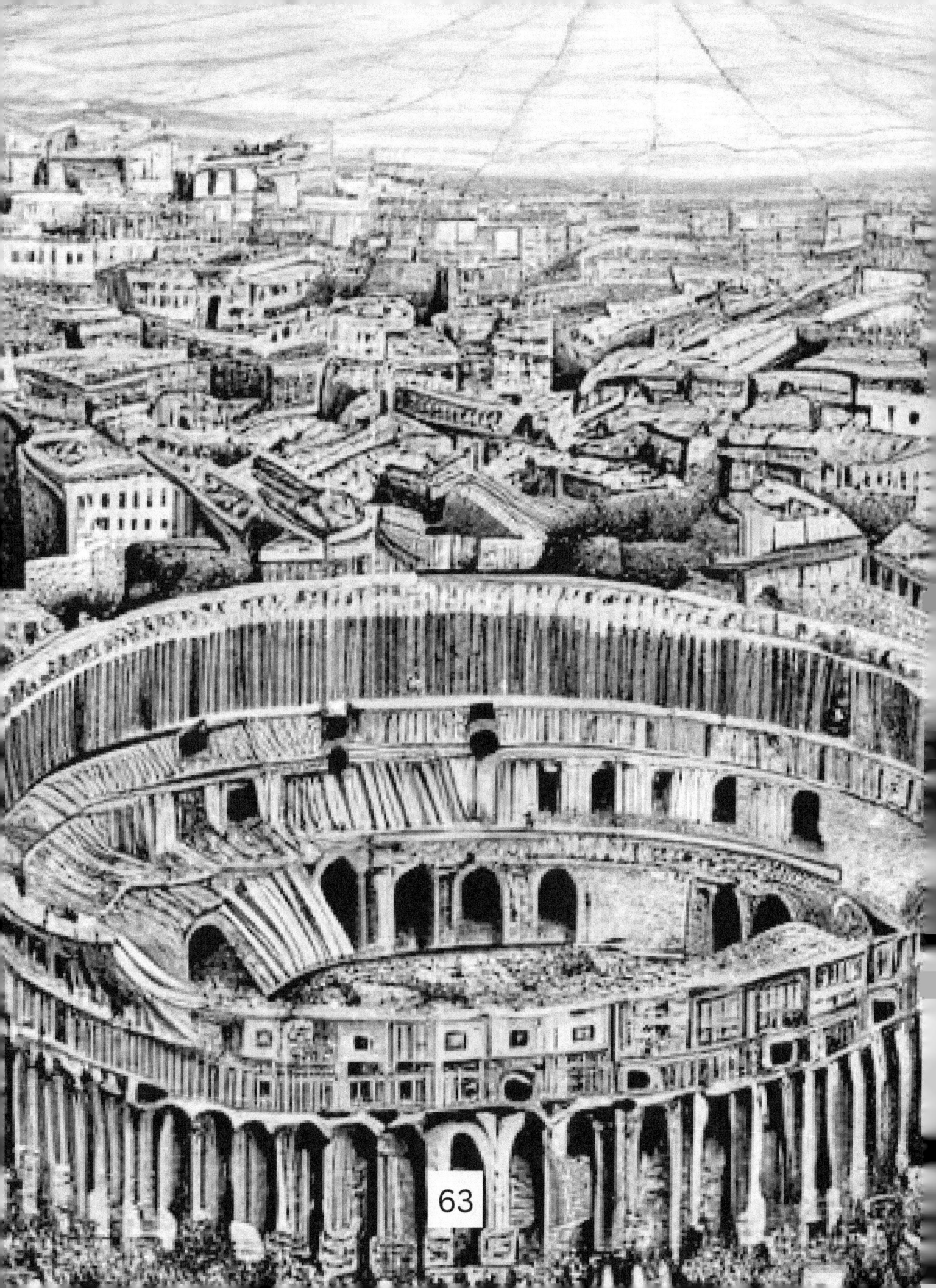

63

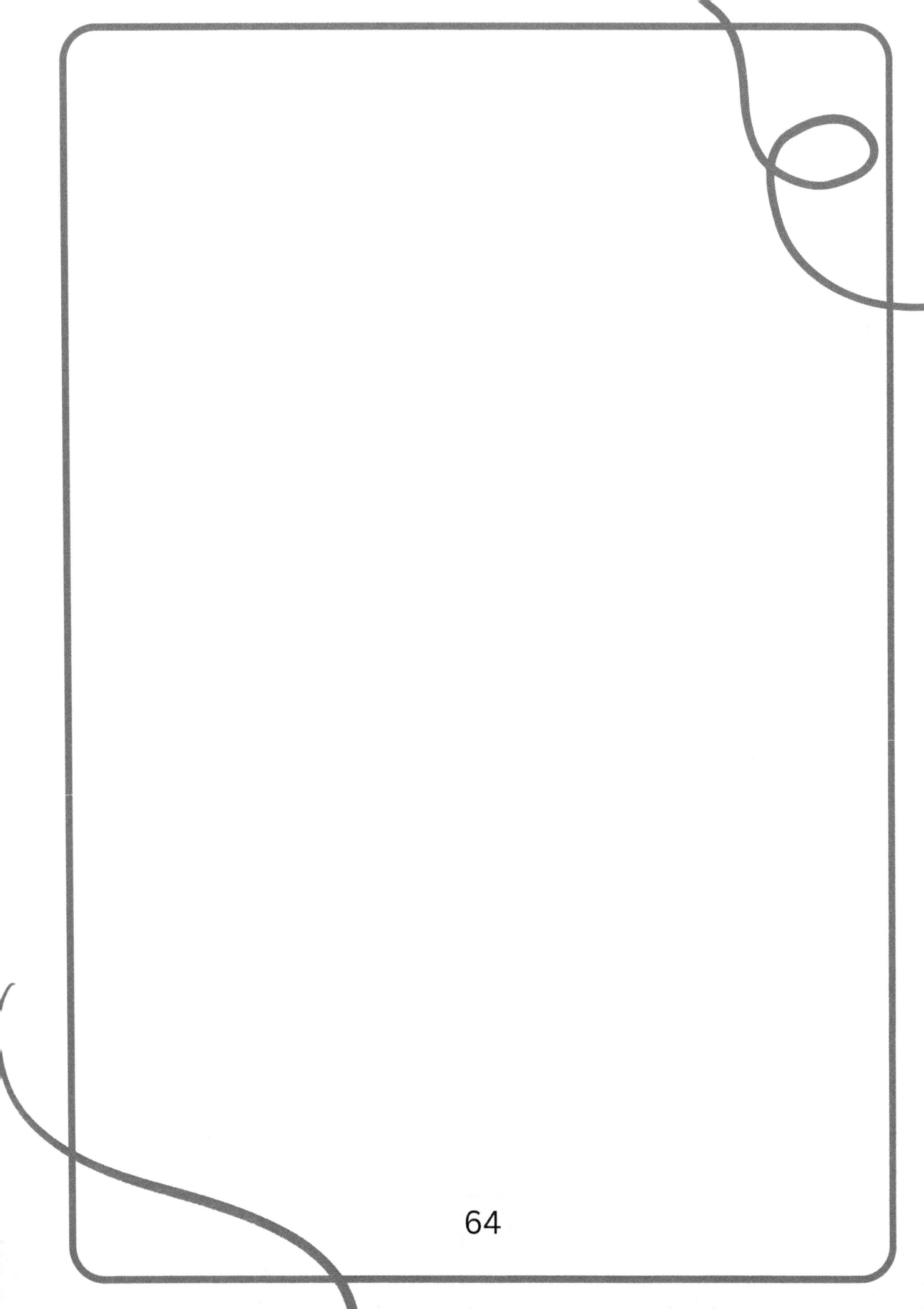

San Francisco, California

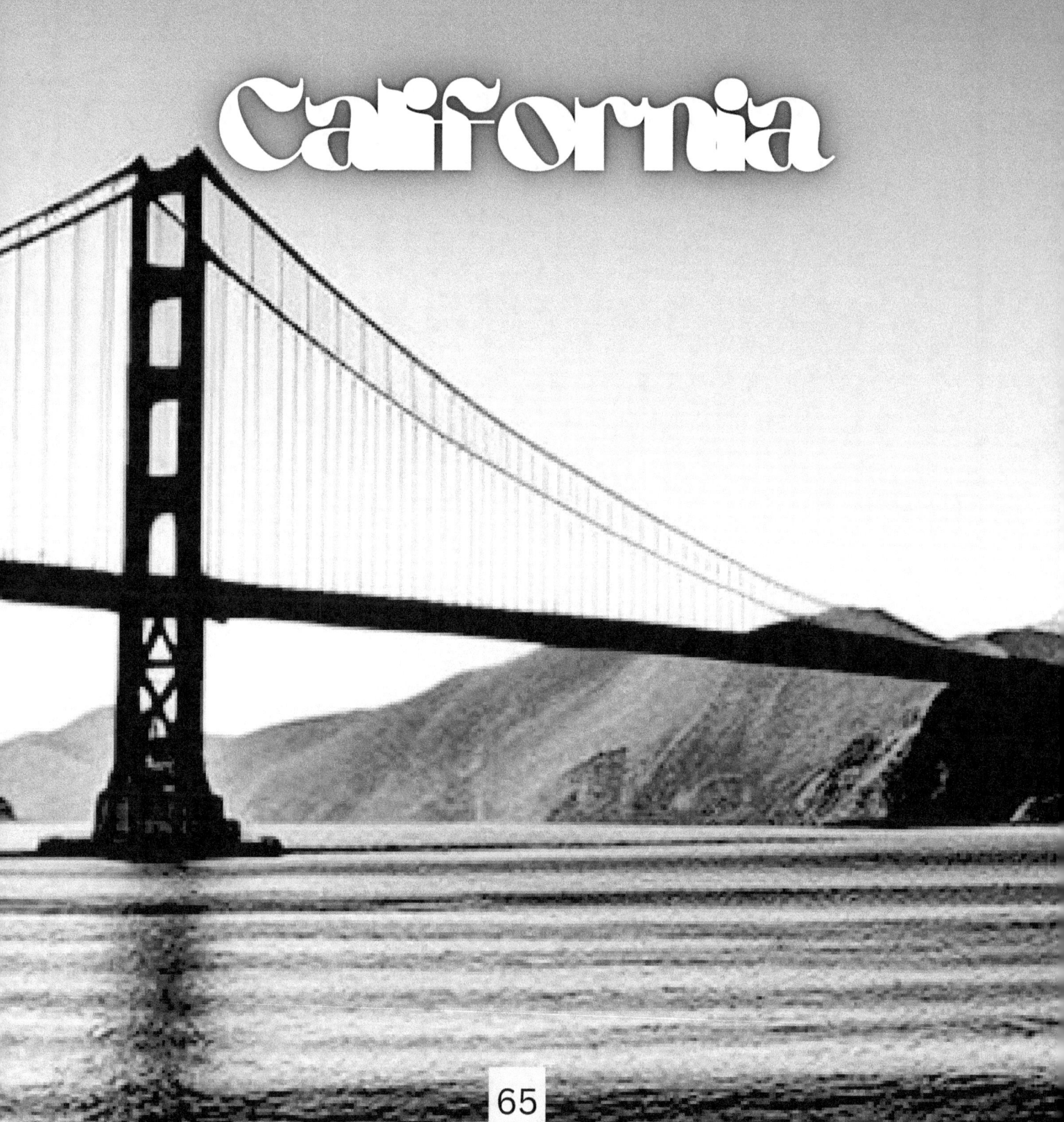

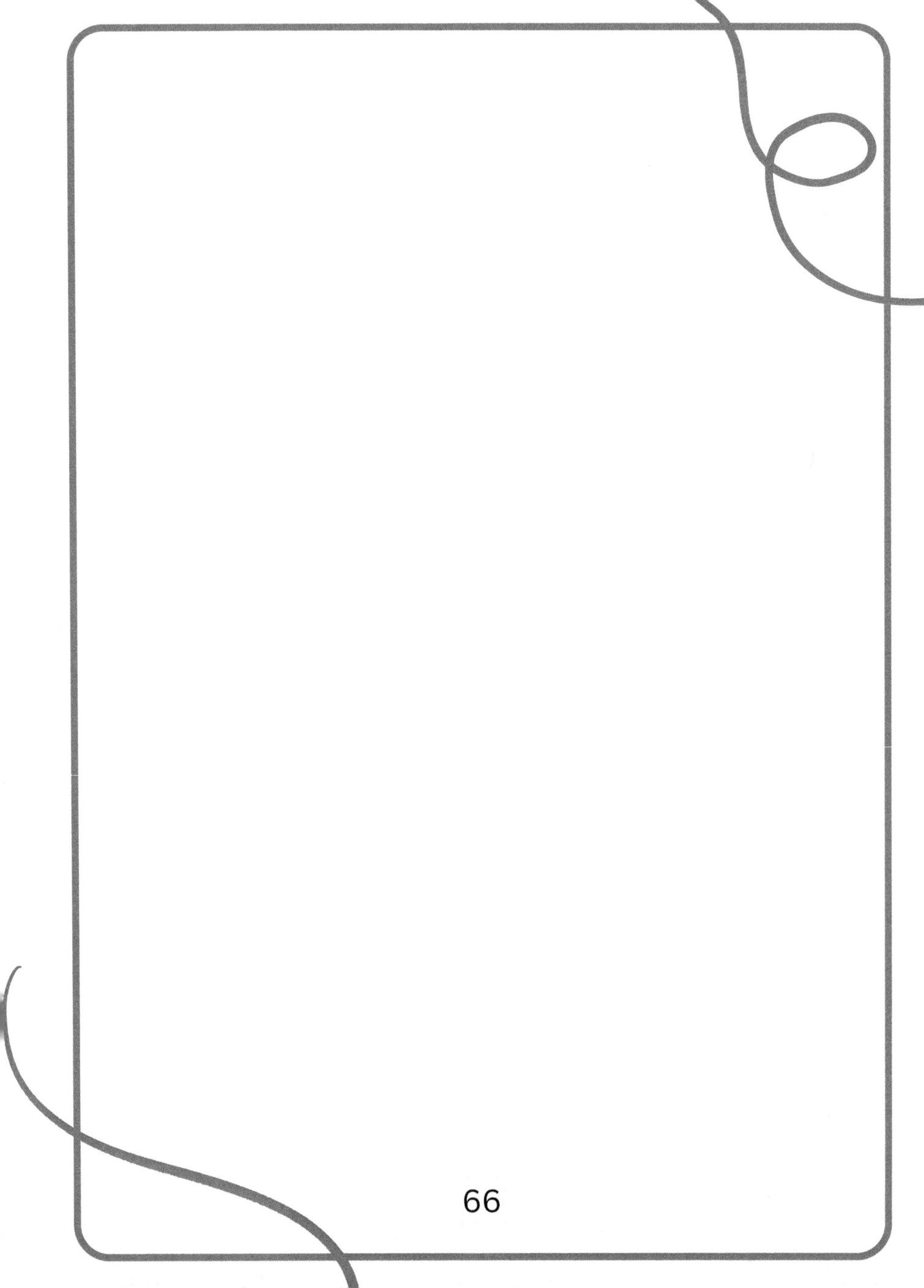

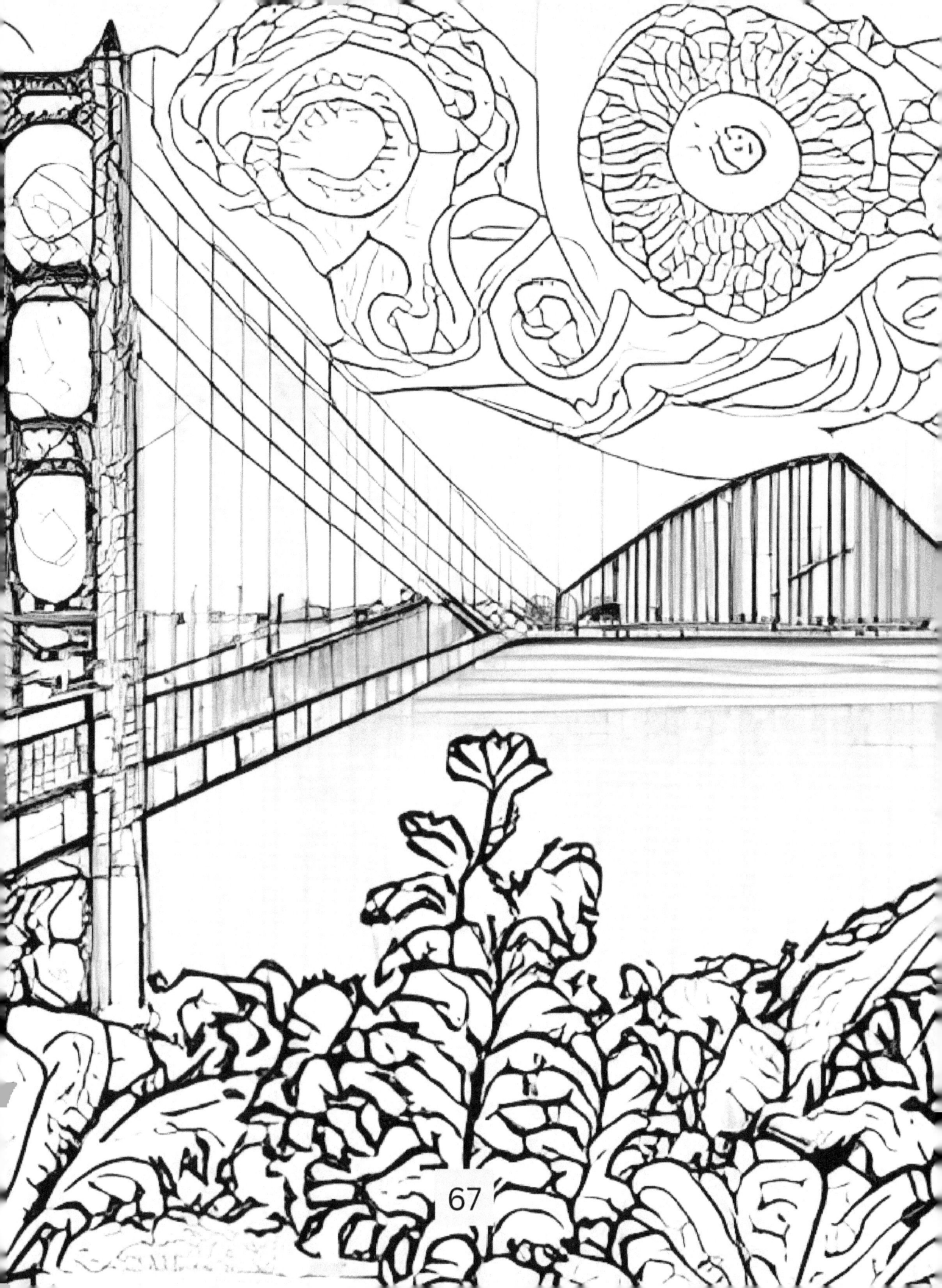

67

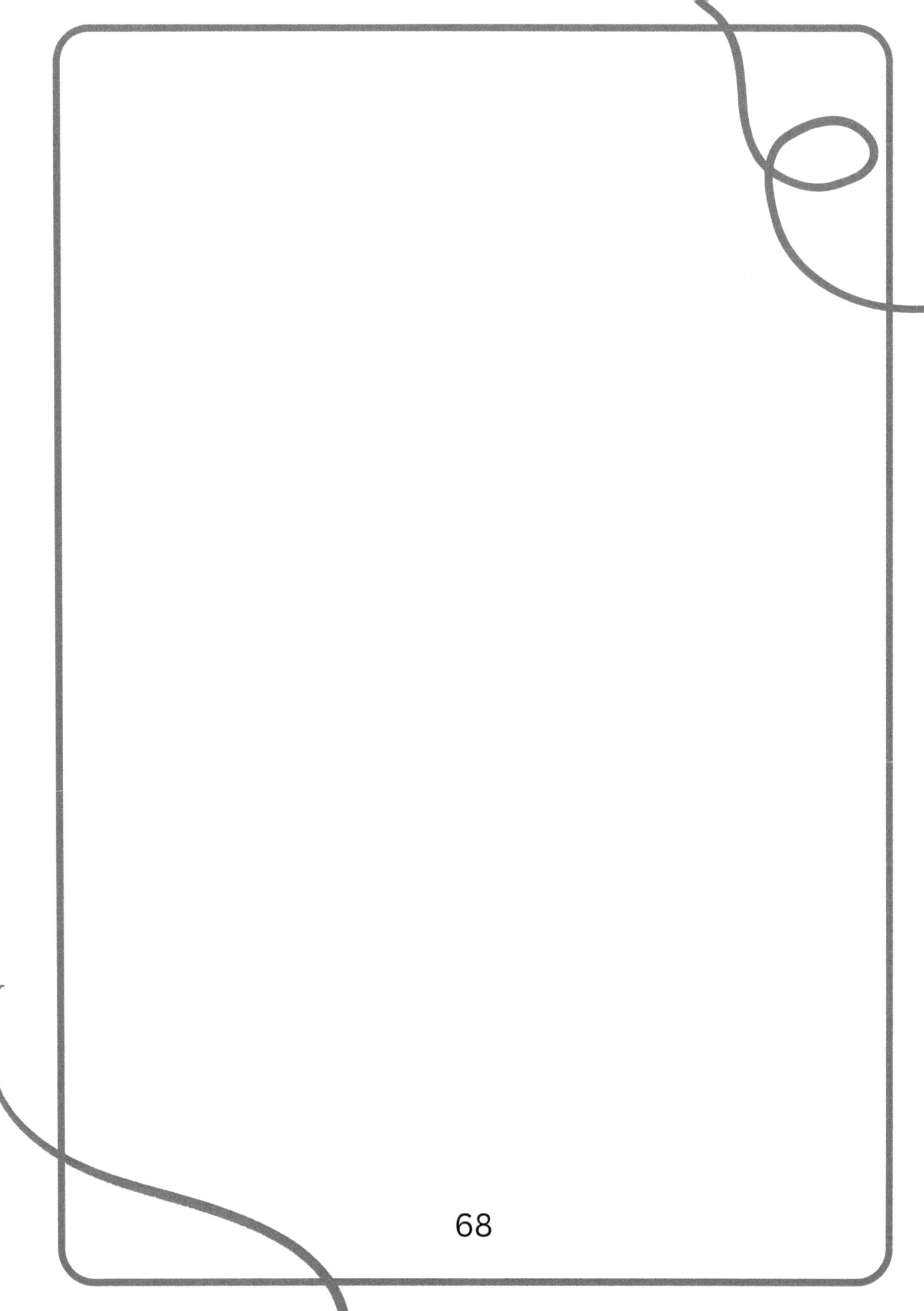

68

Venice, Italy

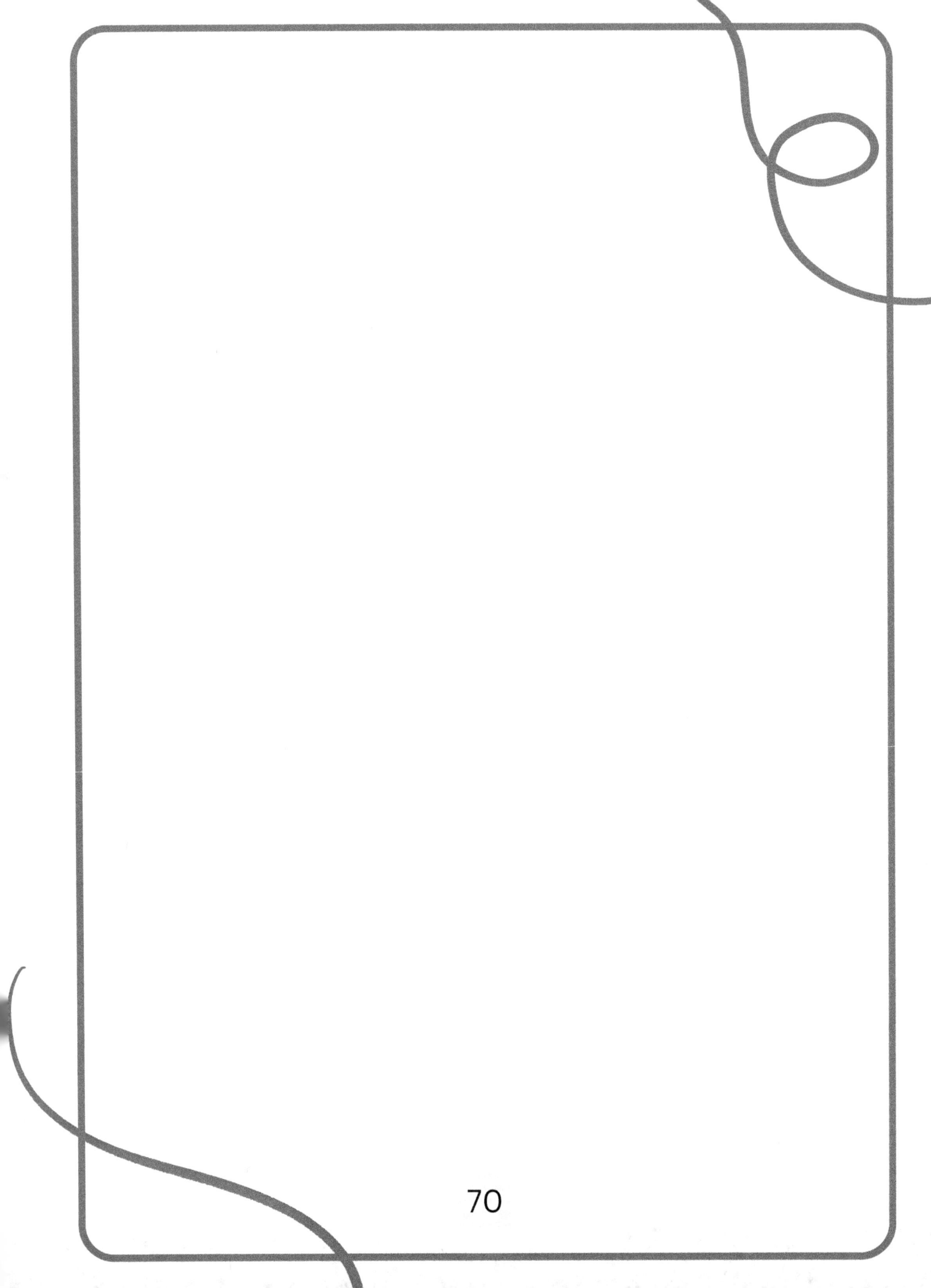

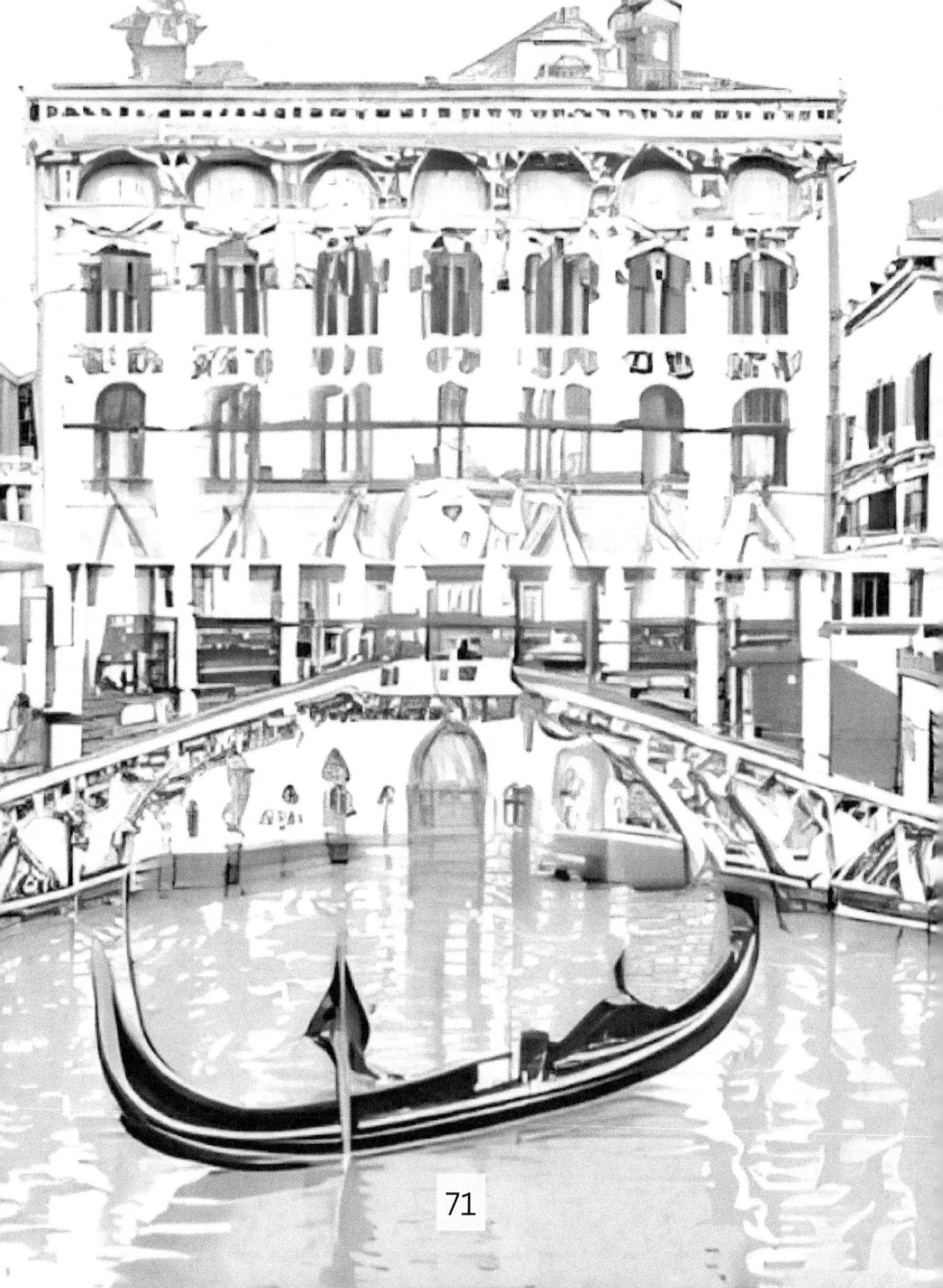

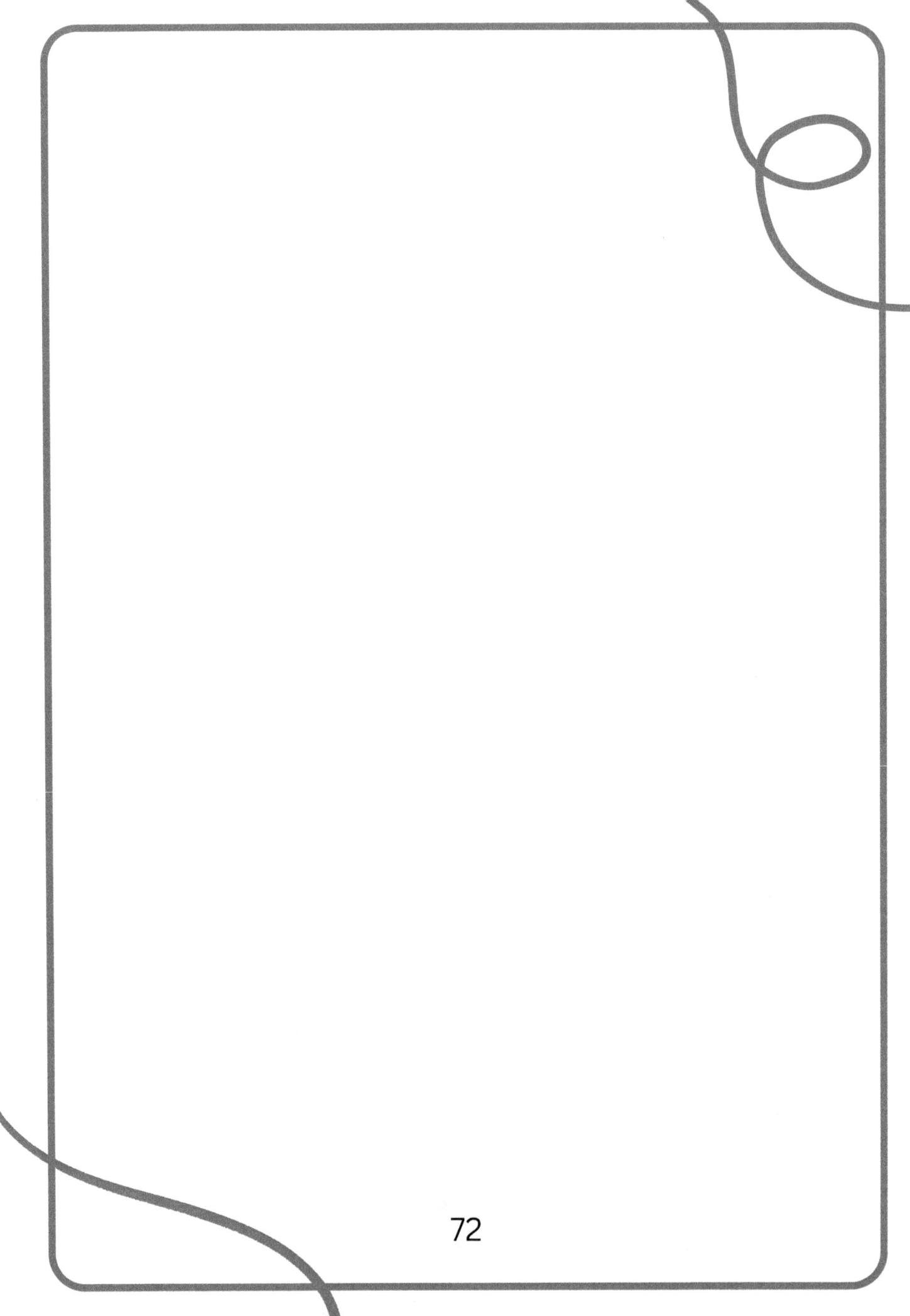

72

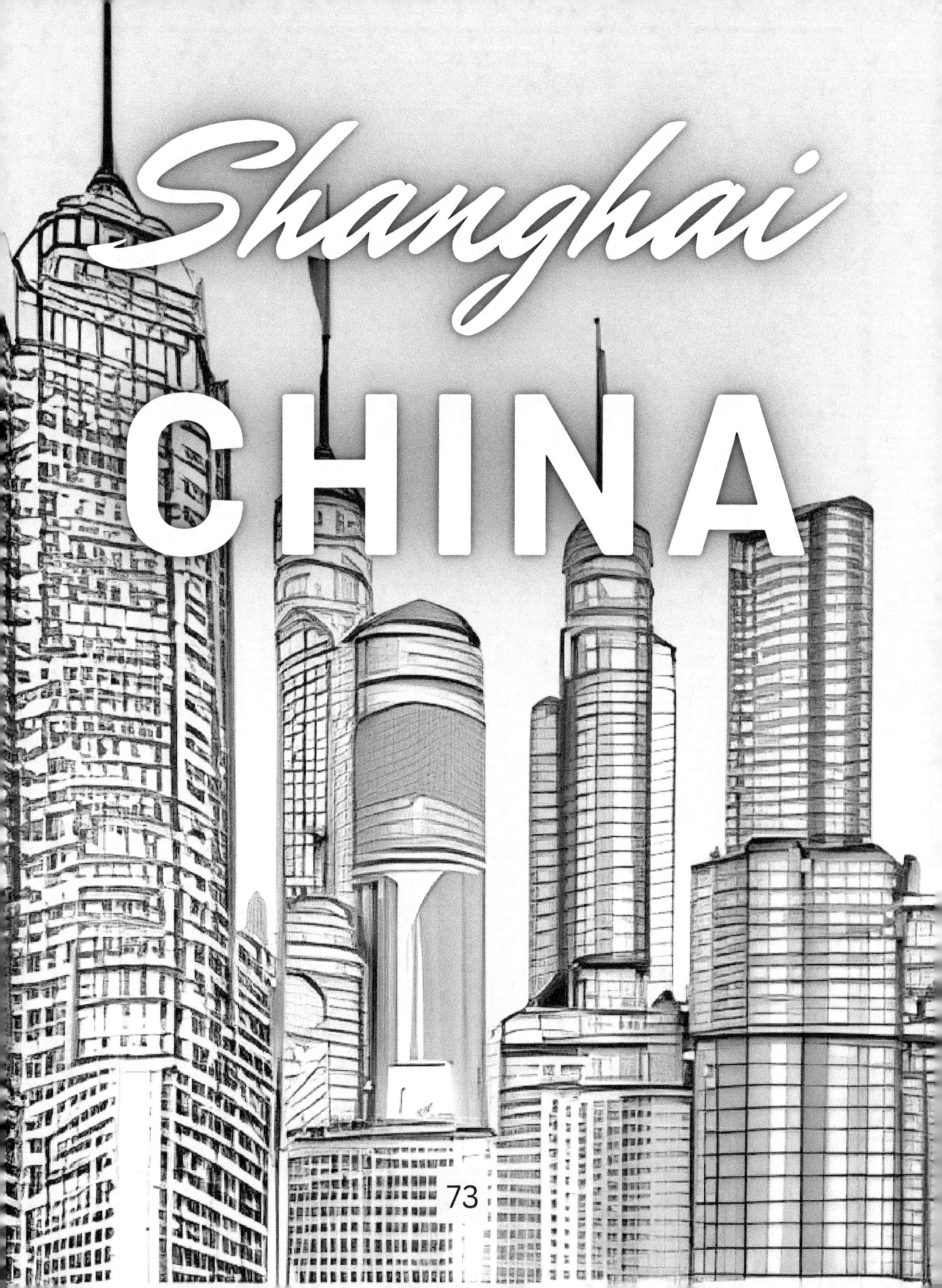

Shanghai

CHINA

73

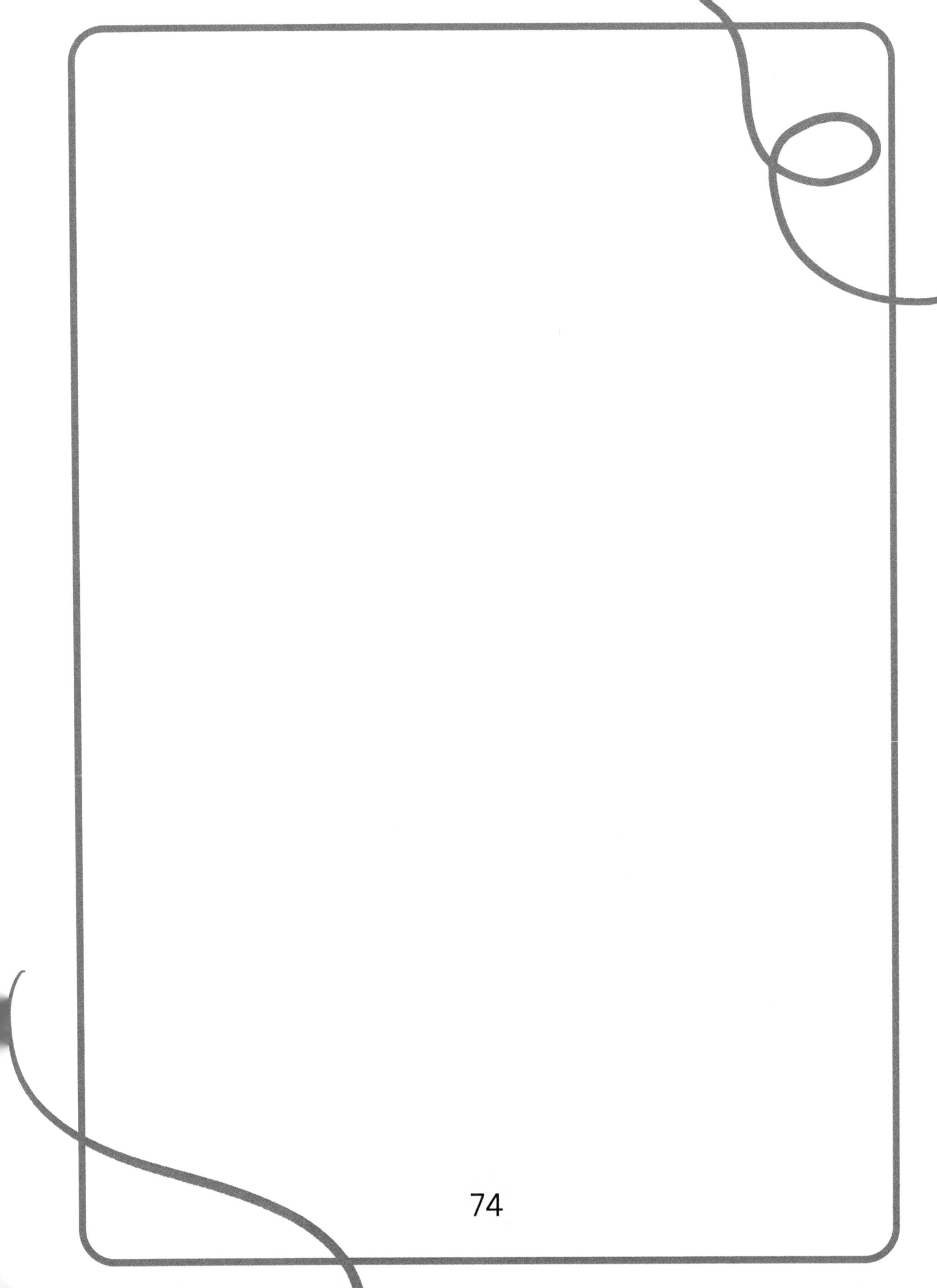

74

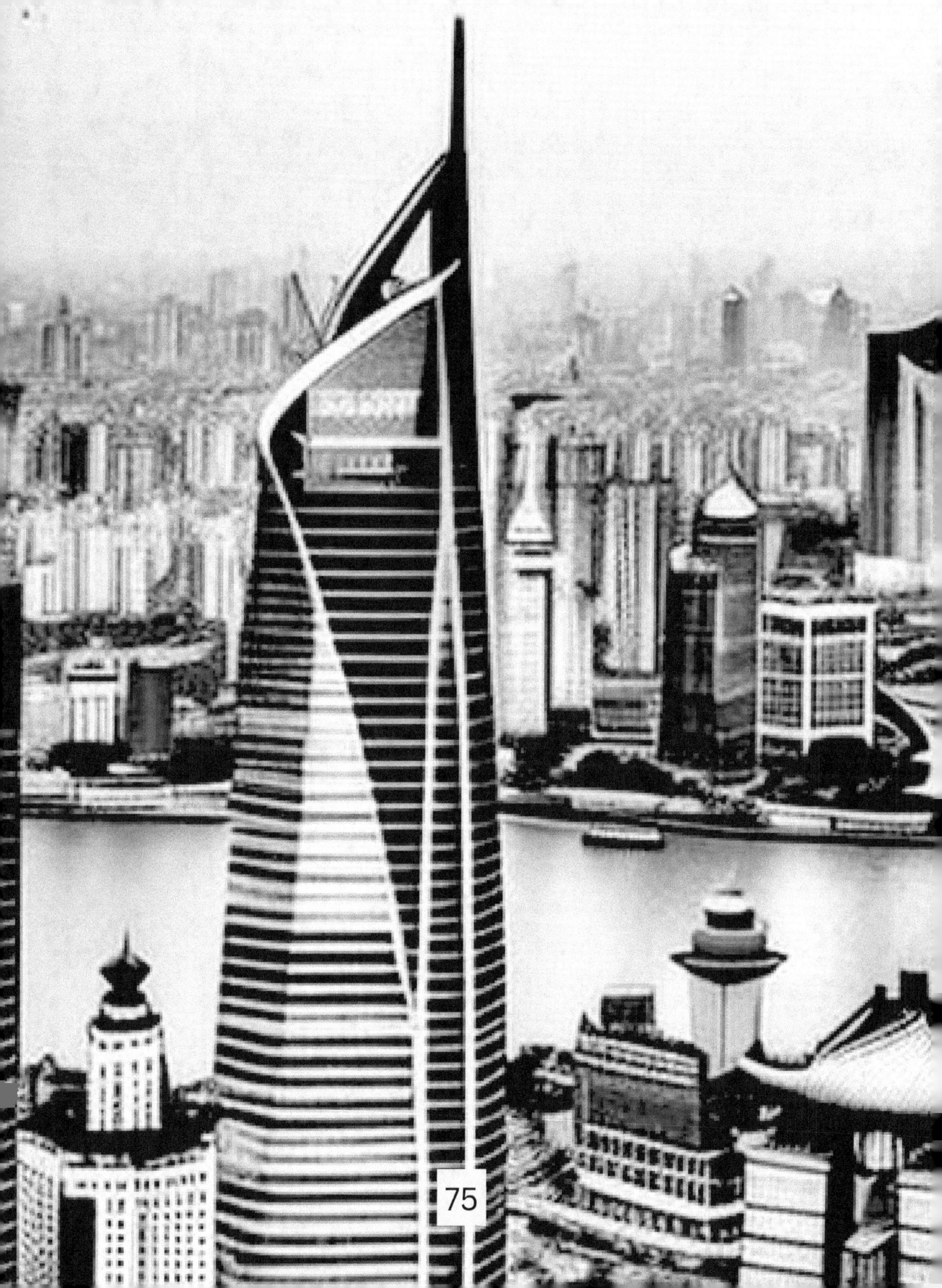

75

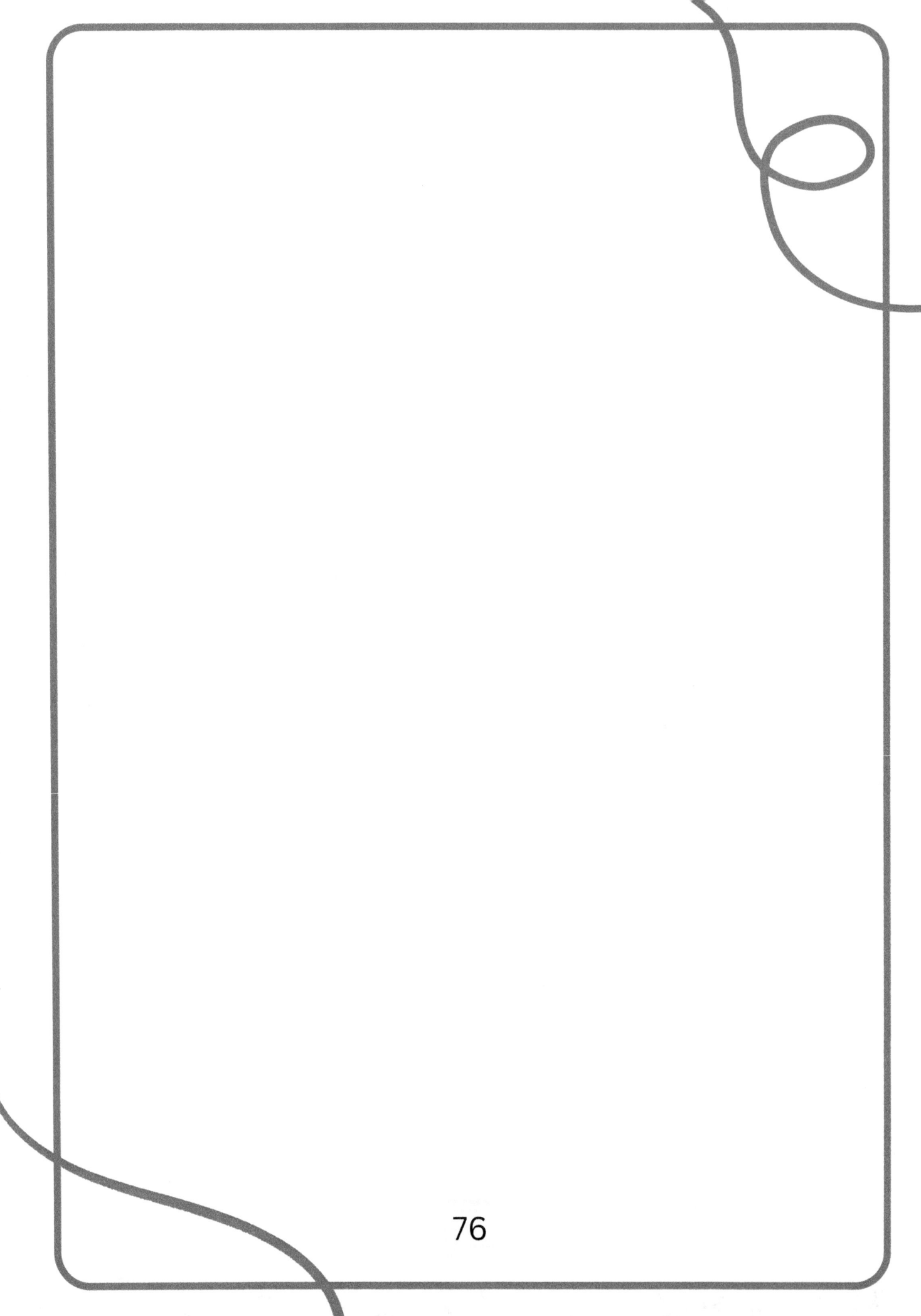

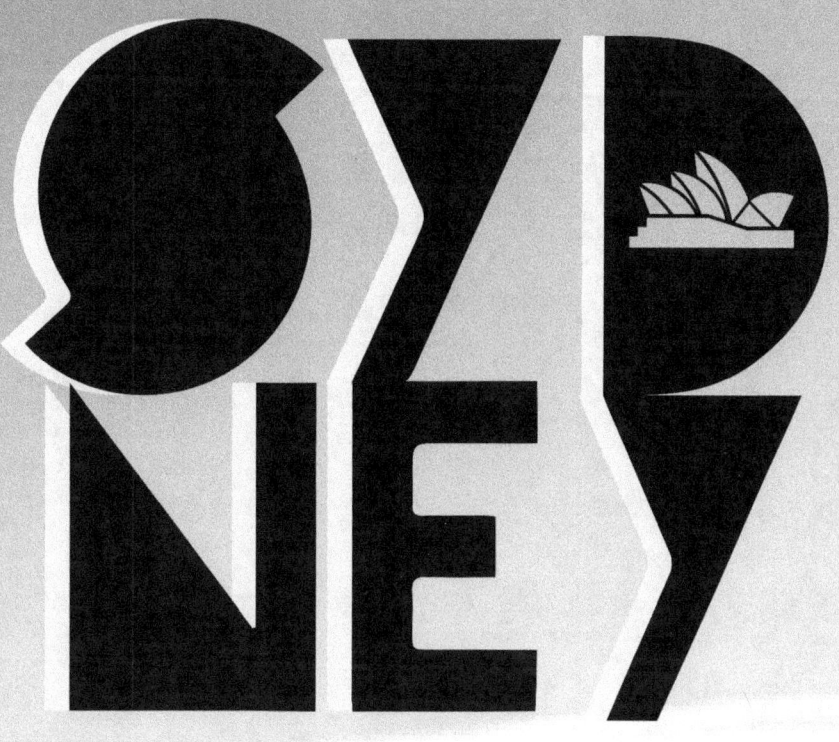

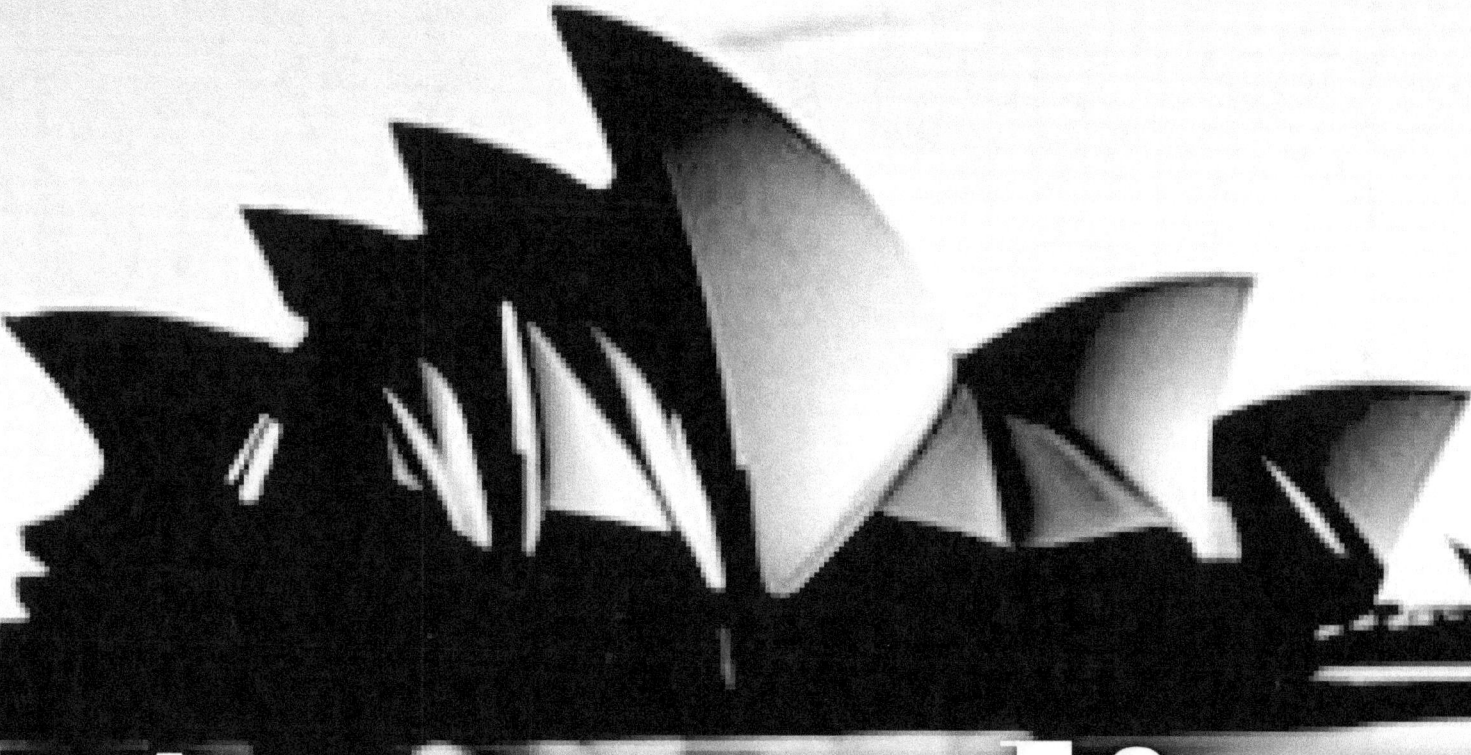

SYDNEY

Australia

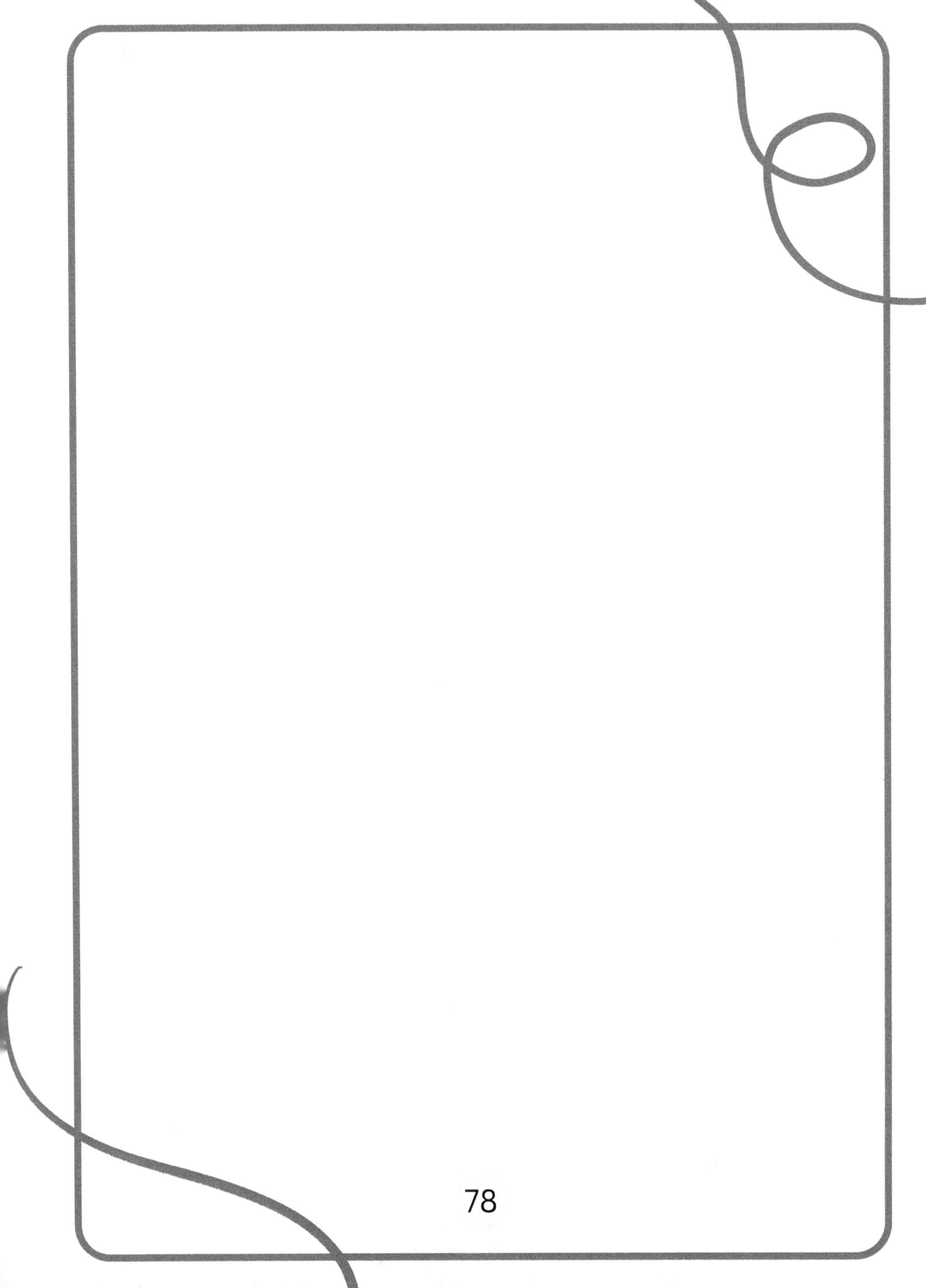

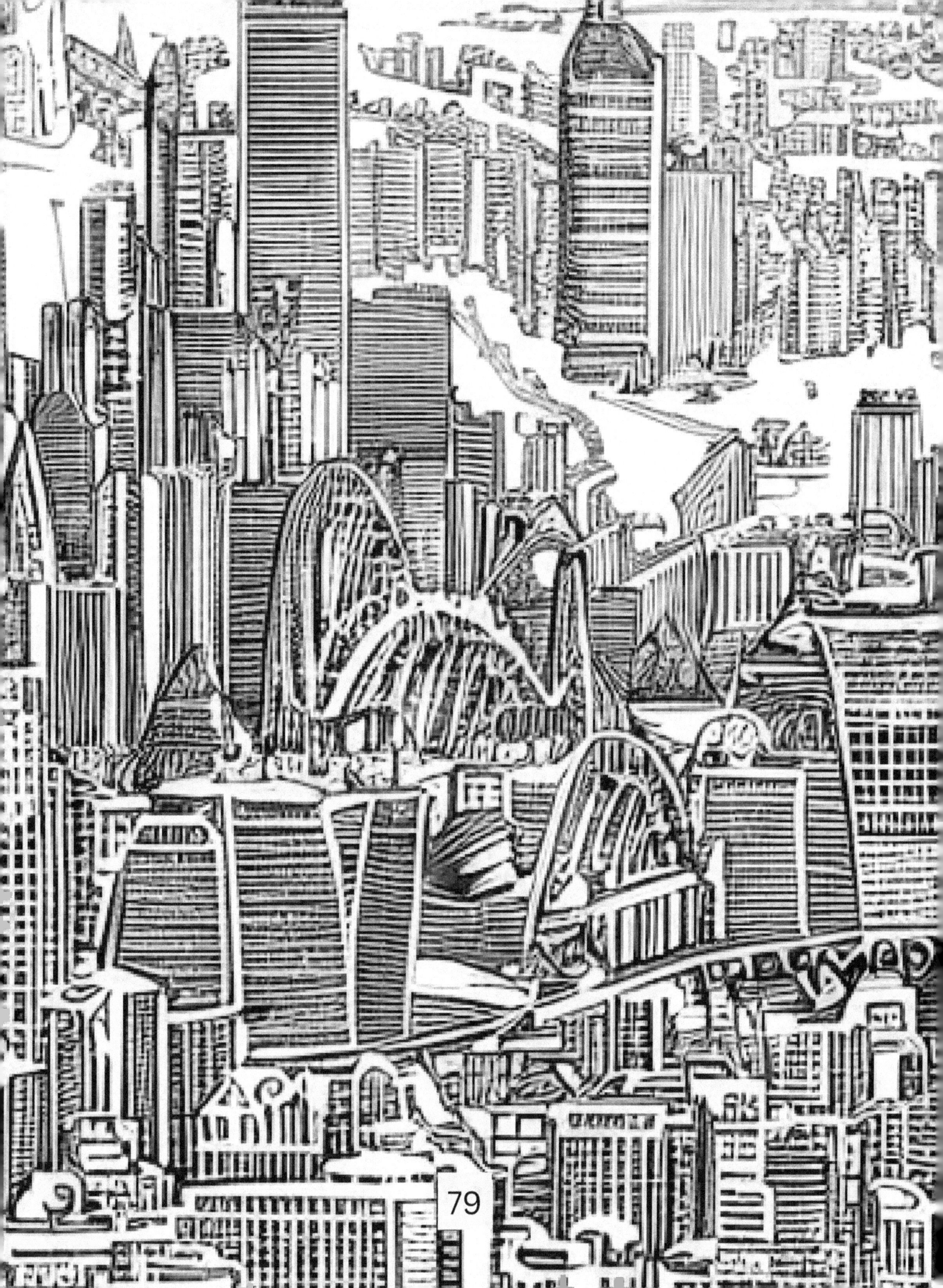

79

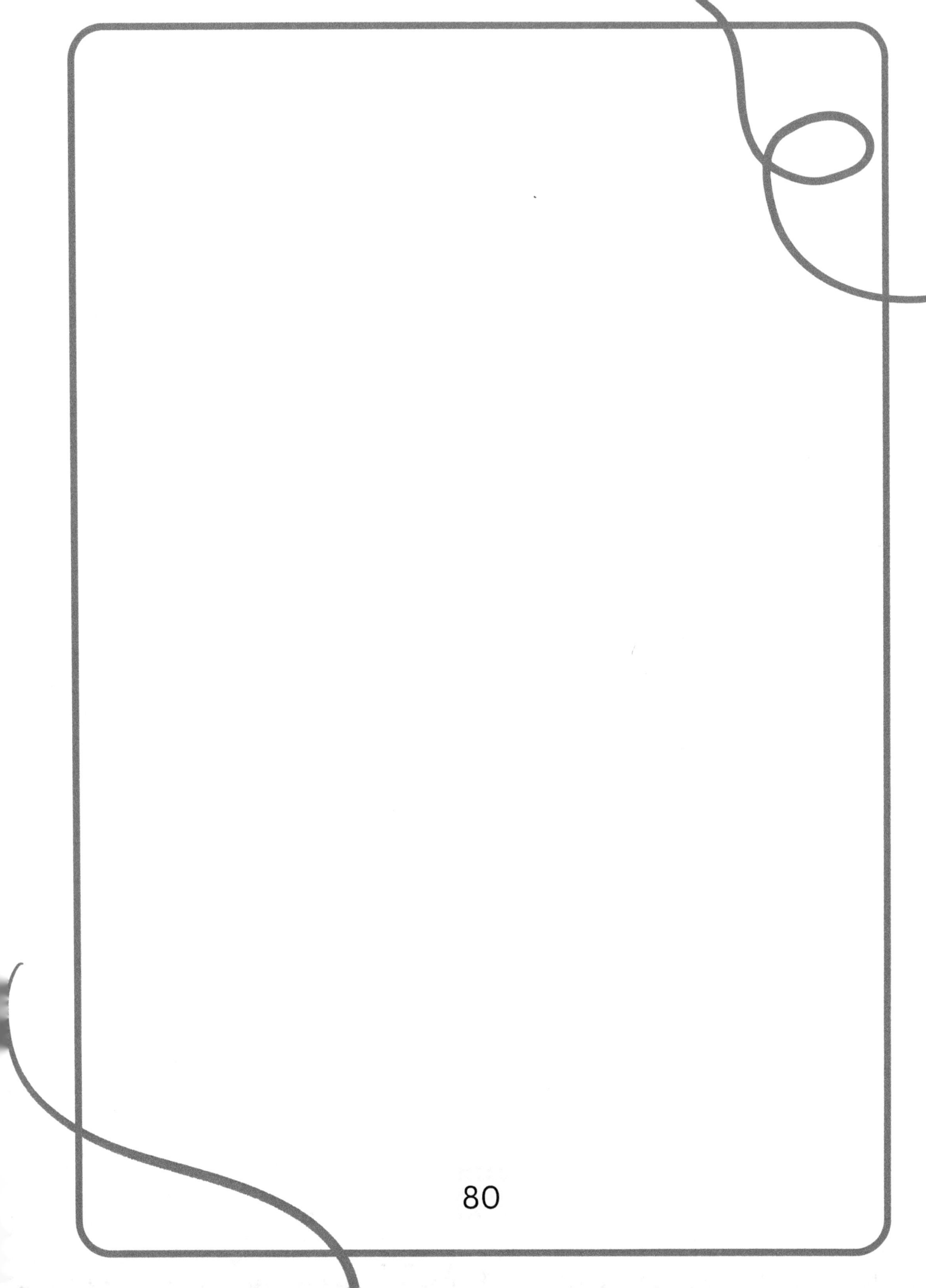

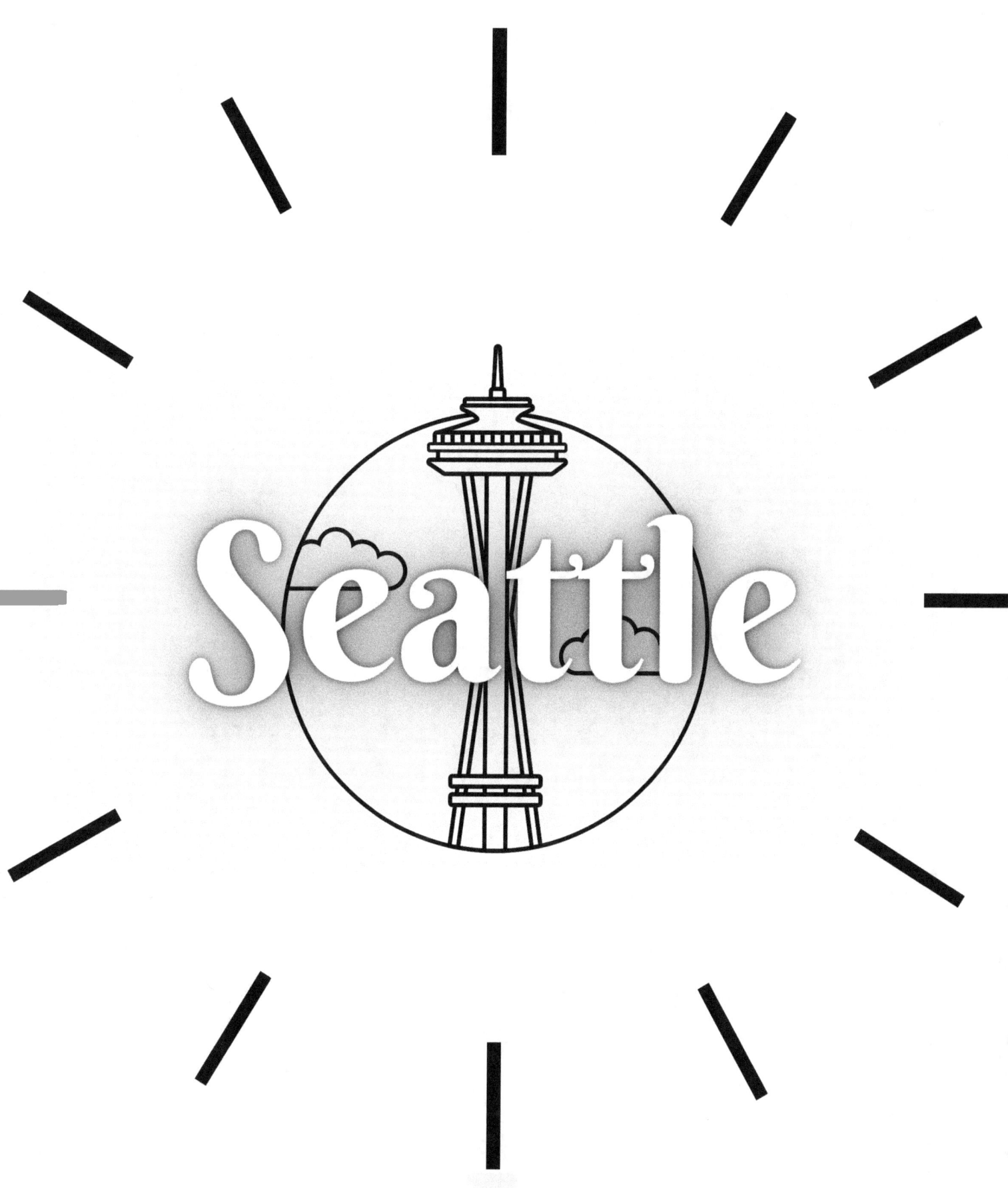

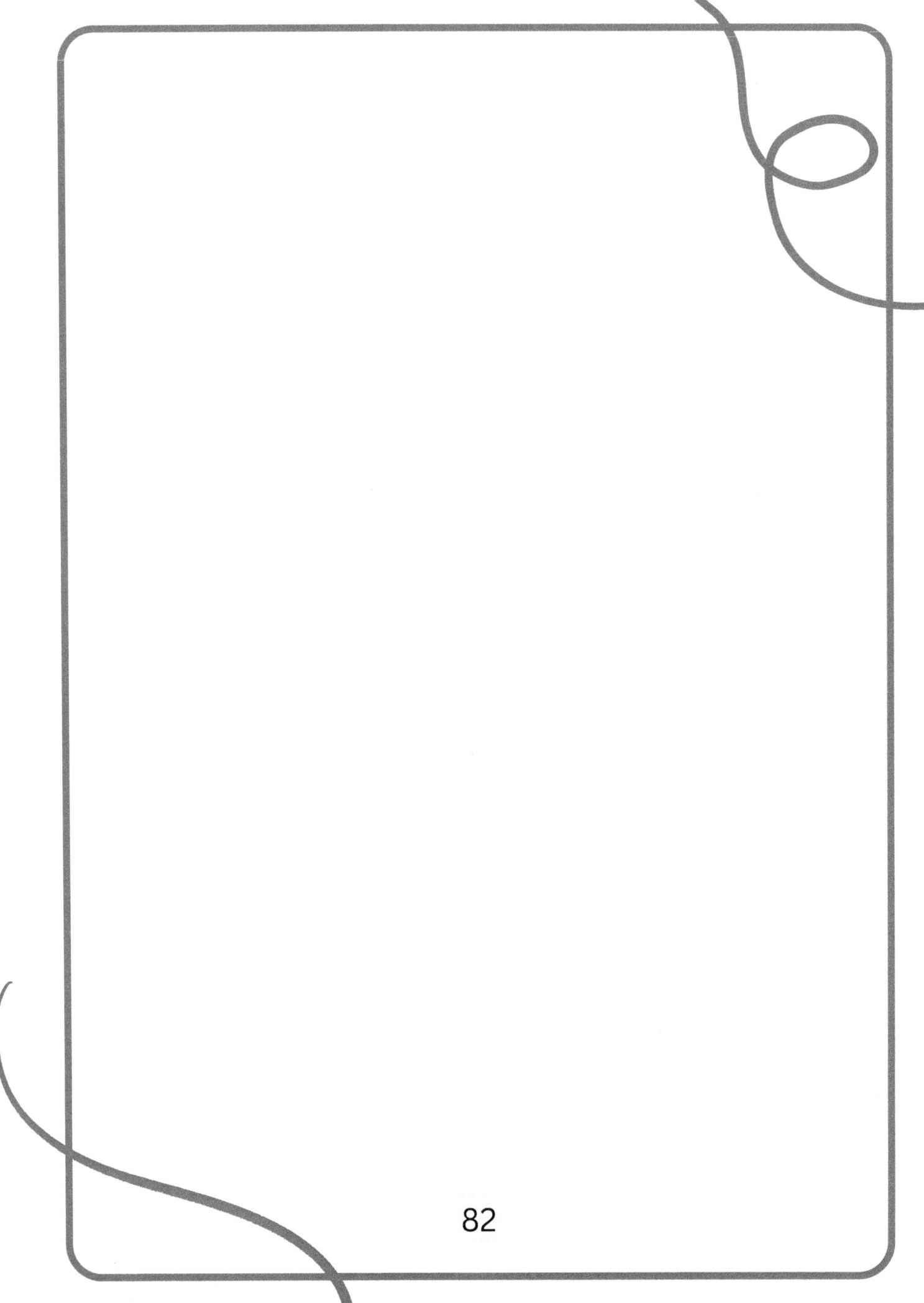

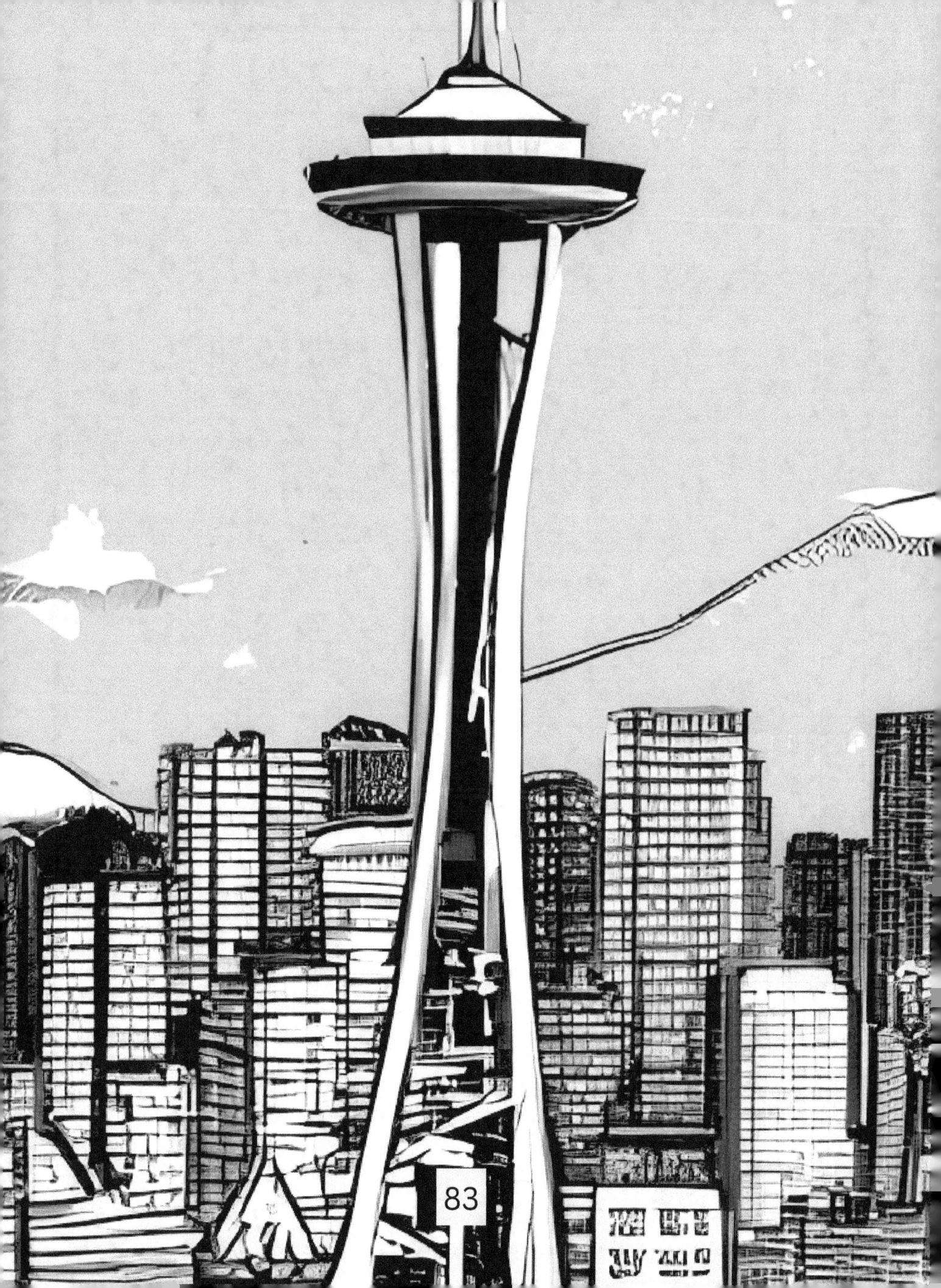

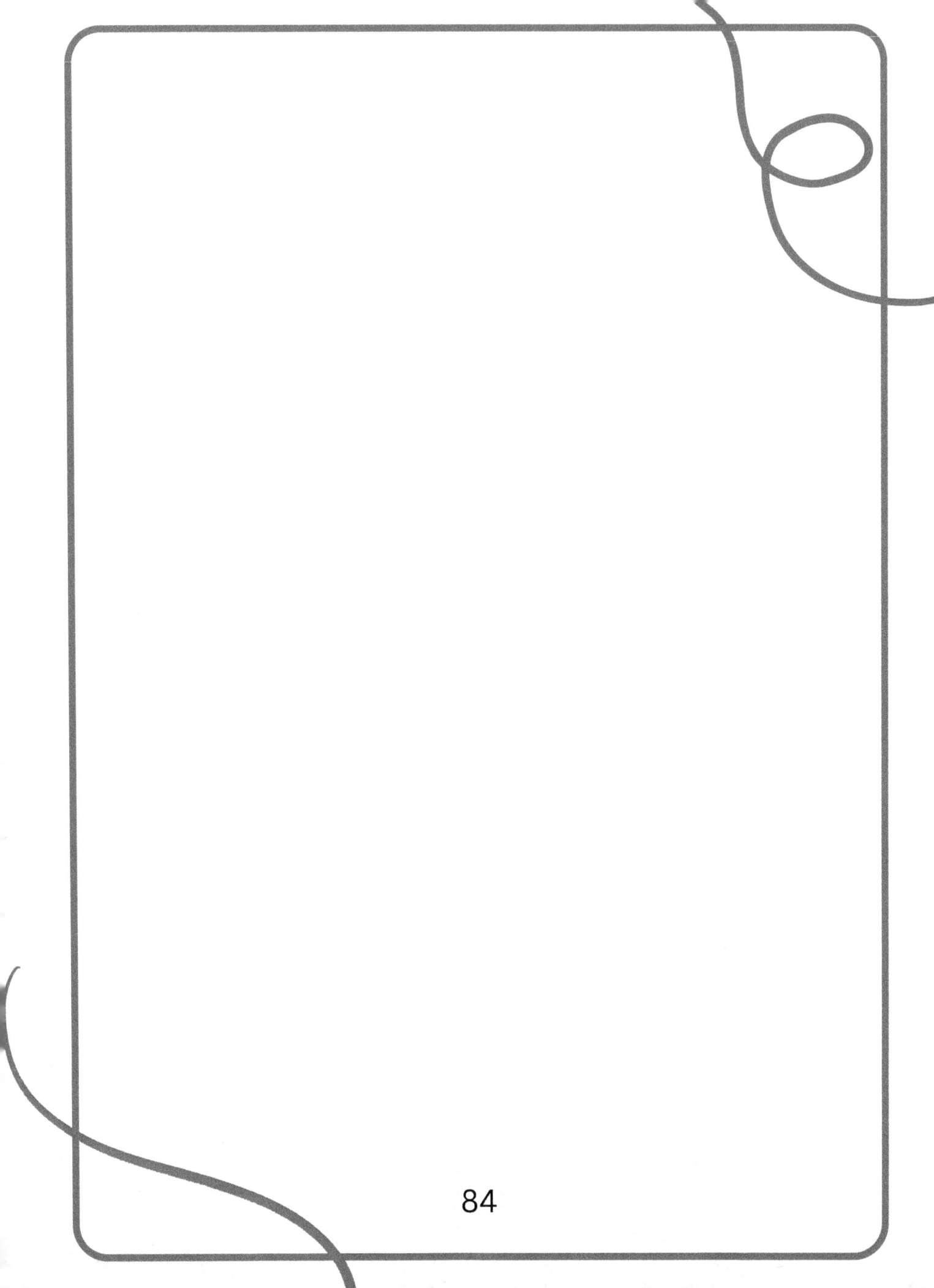

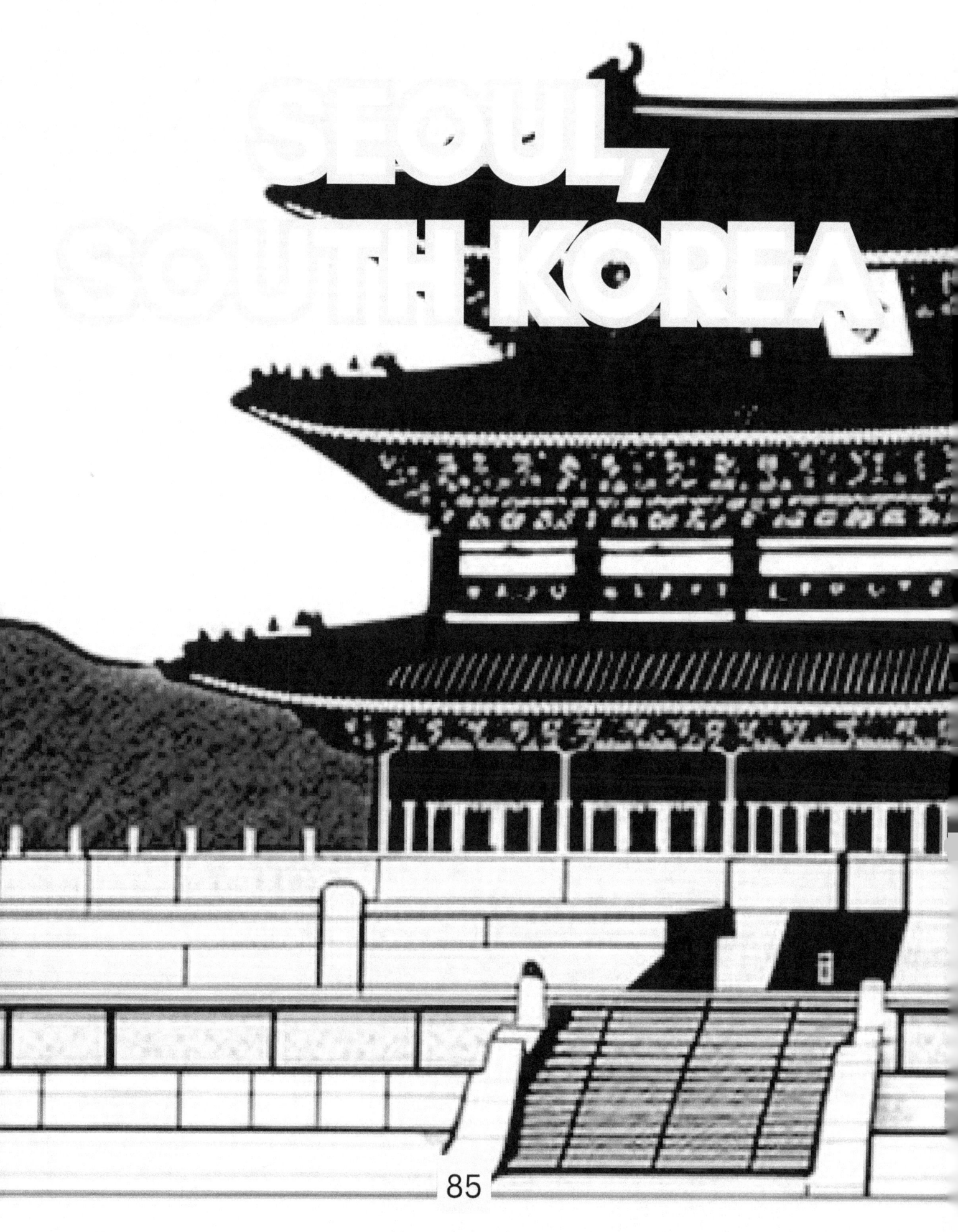

SEOUL, SOUTH KOREA

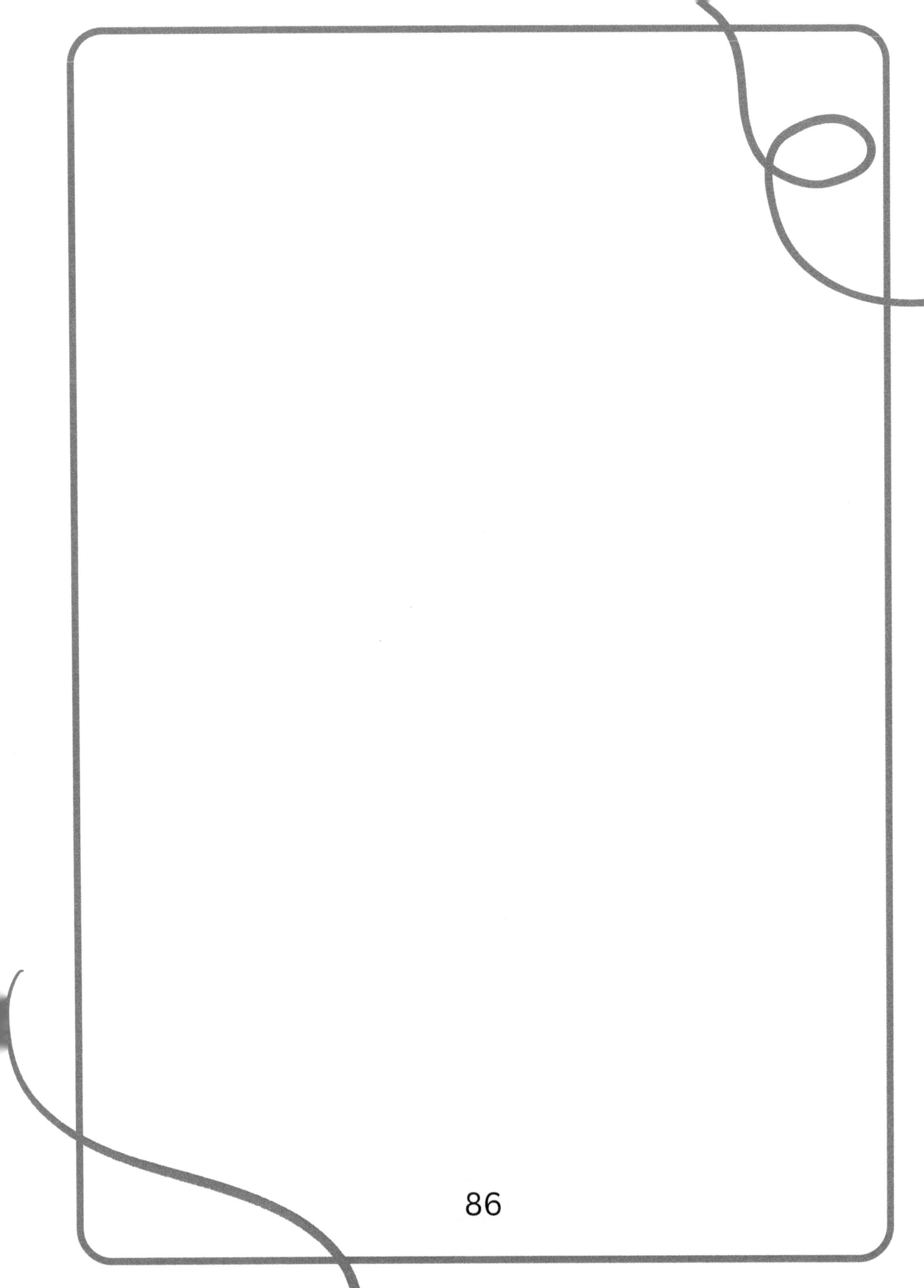

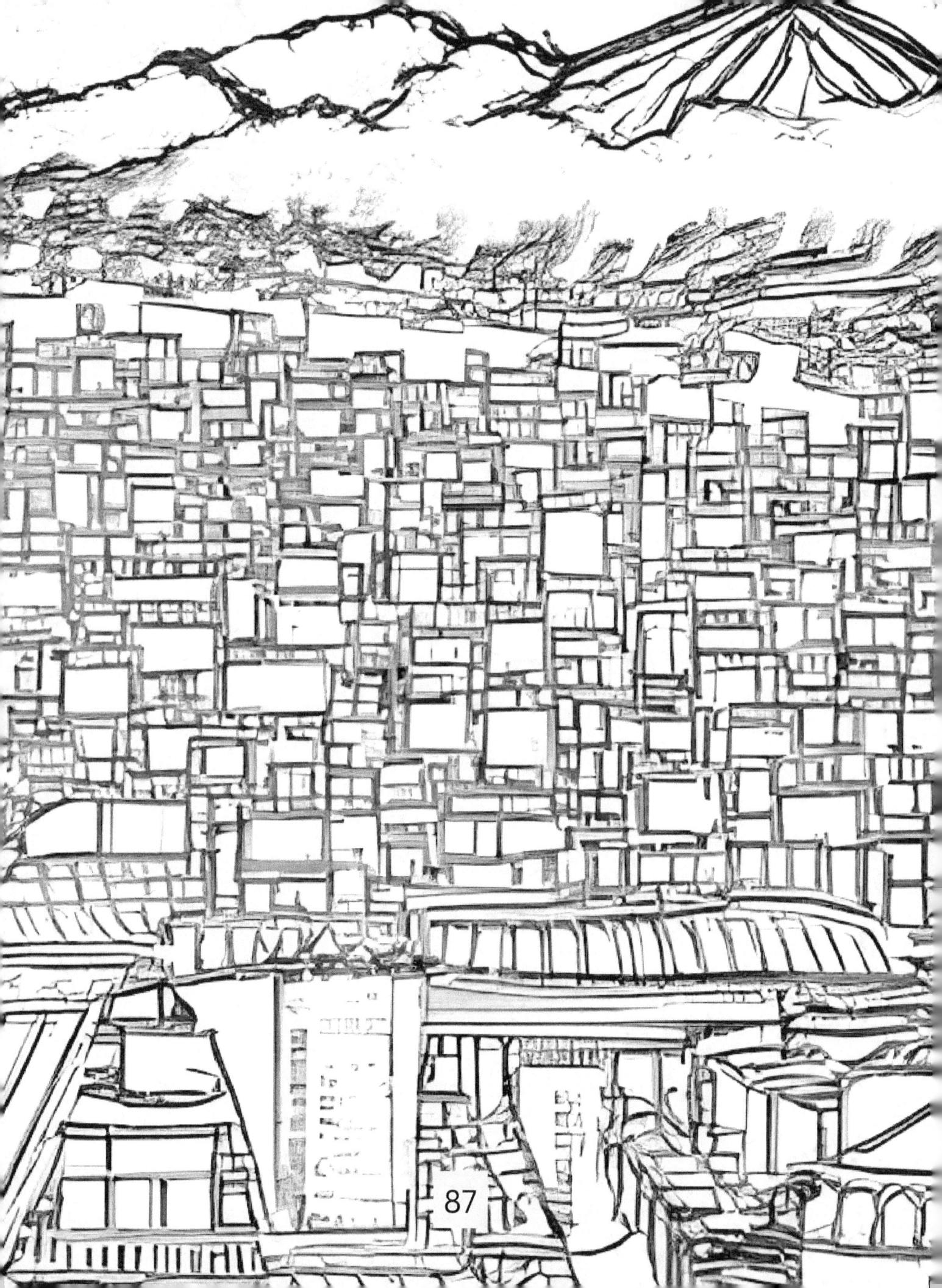

87

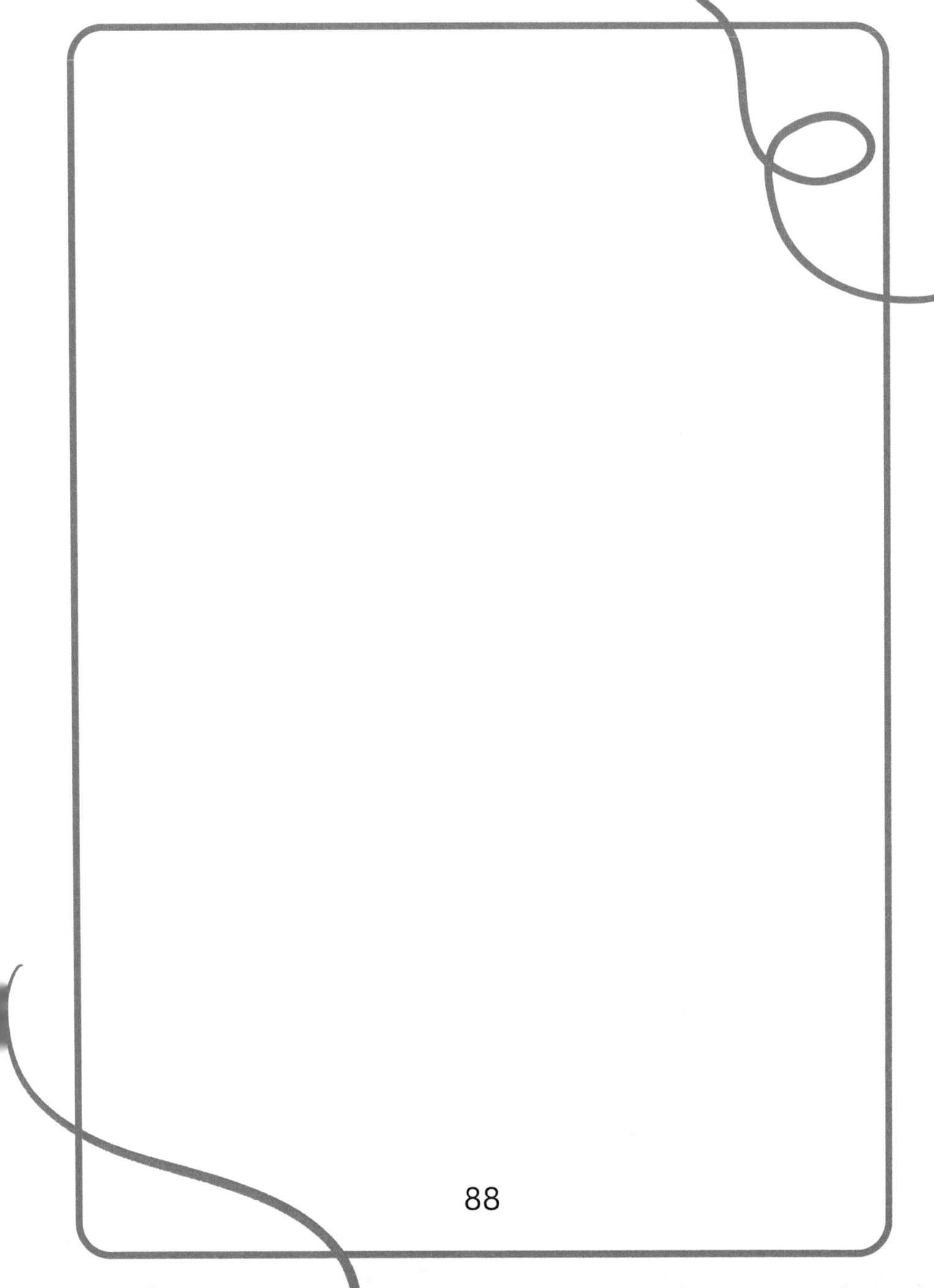

London, England

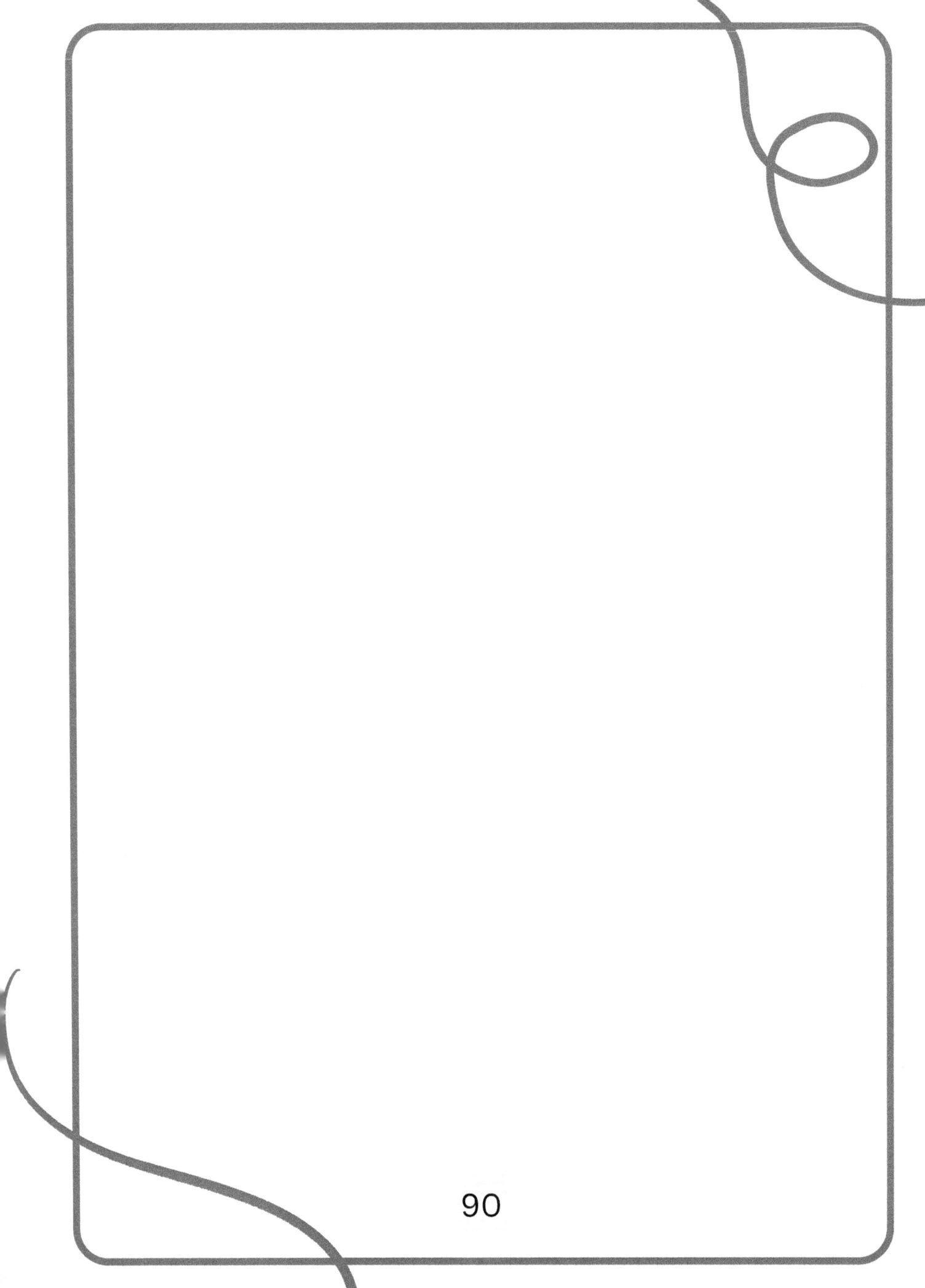

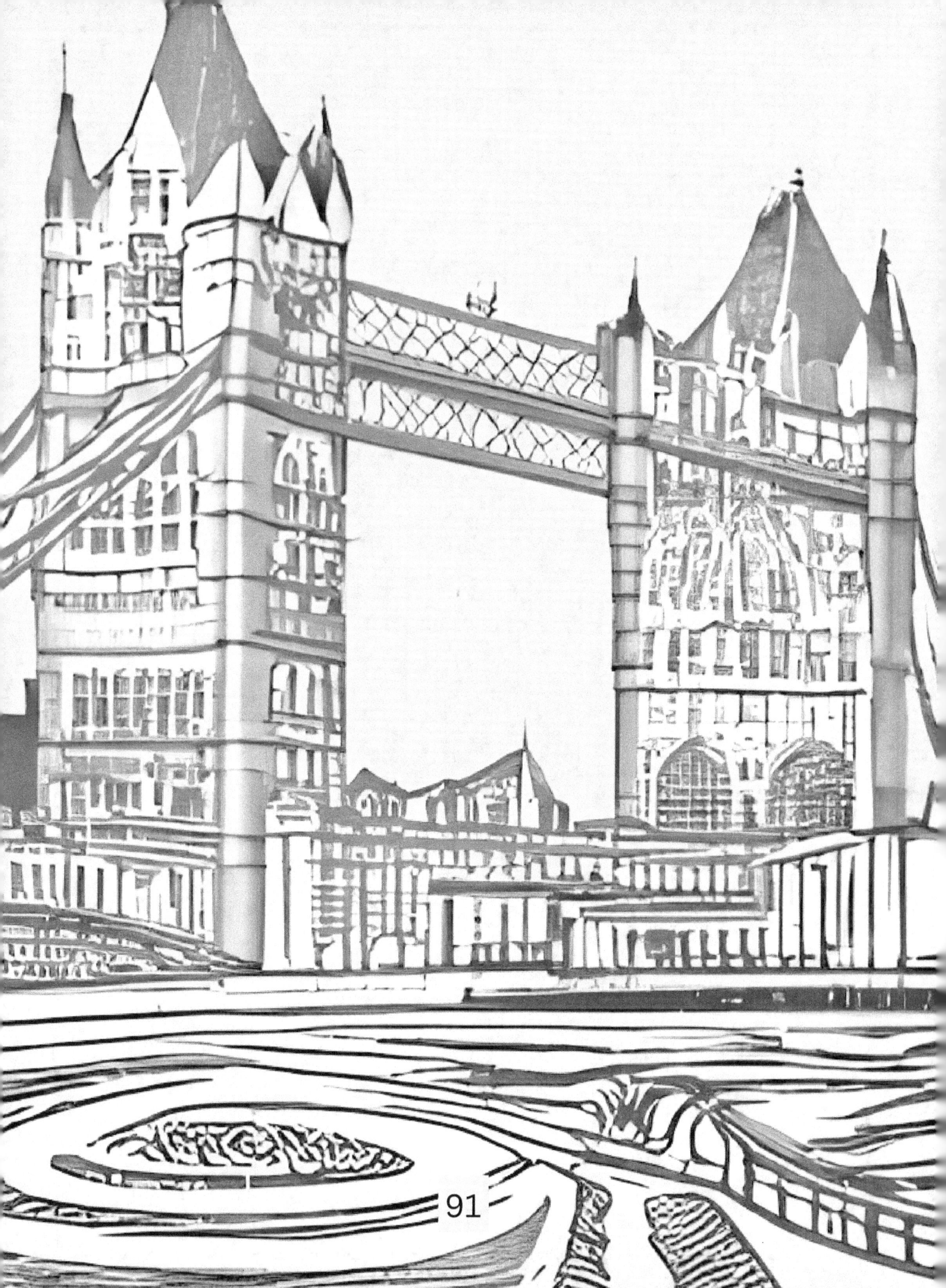

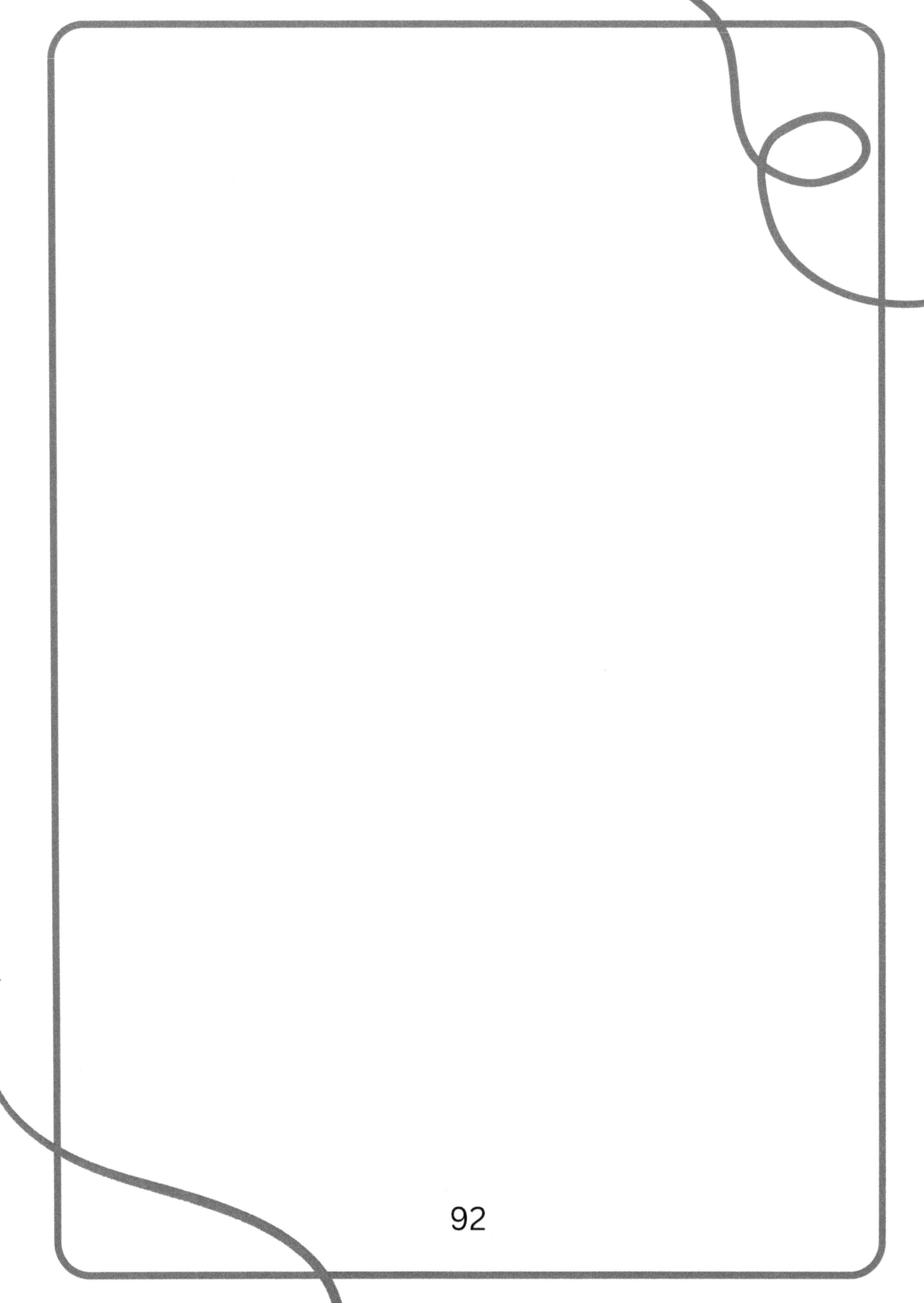

Miami,
Florida

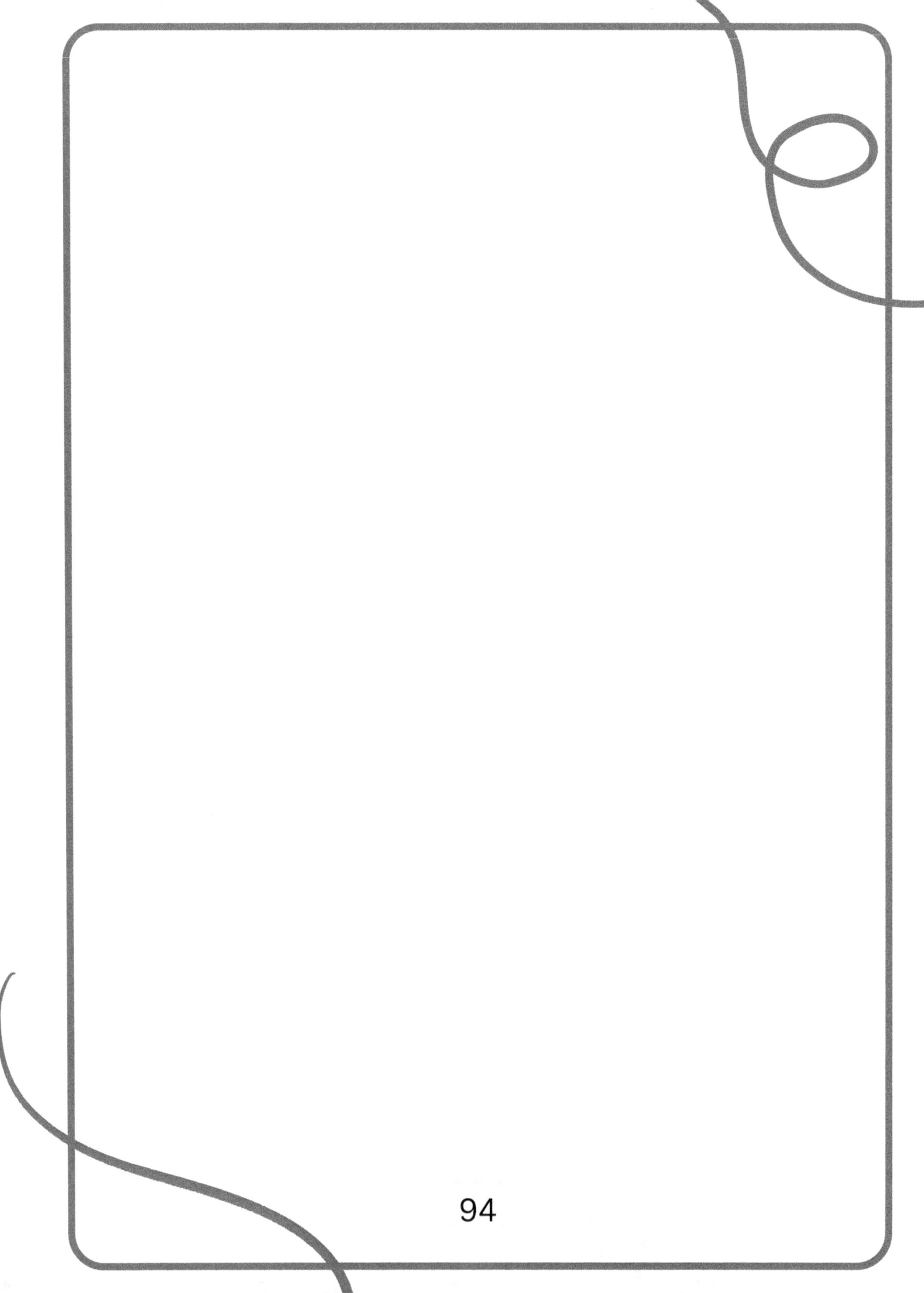

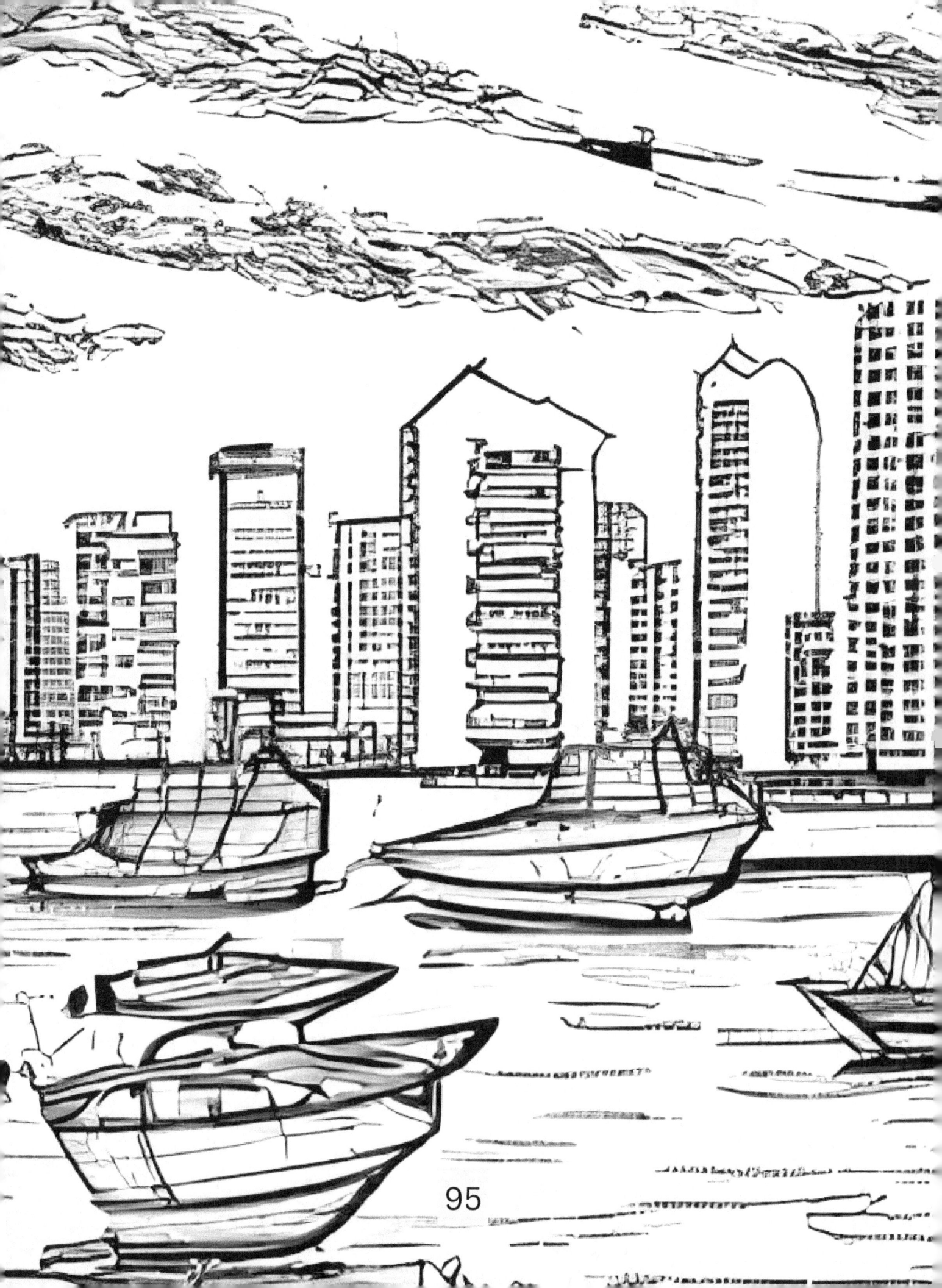

95

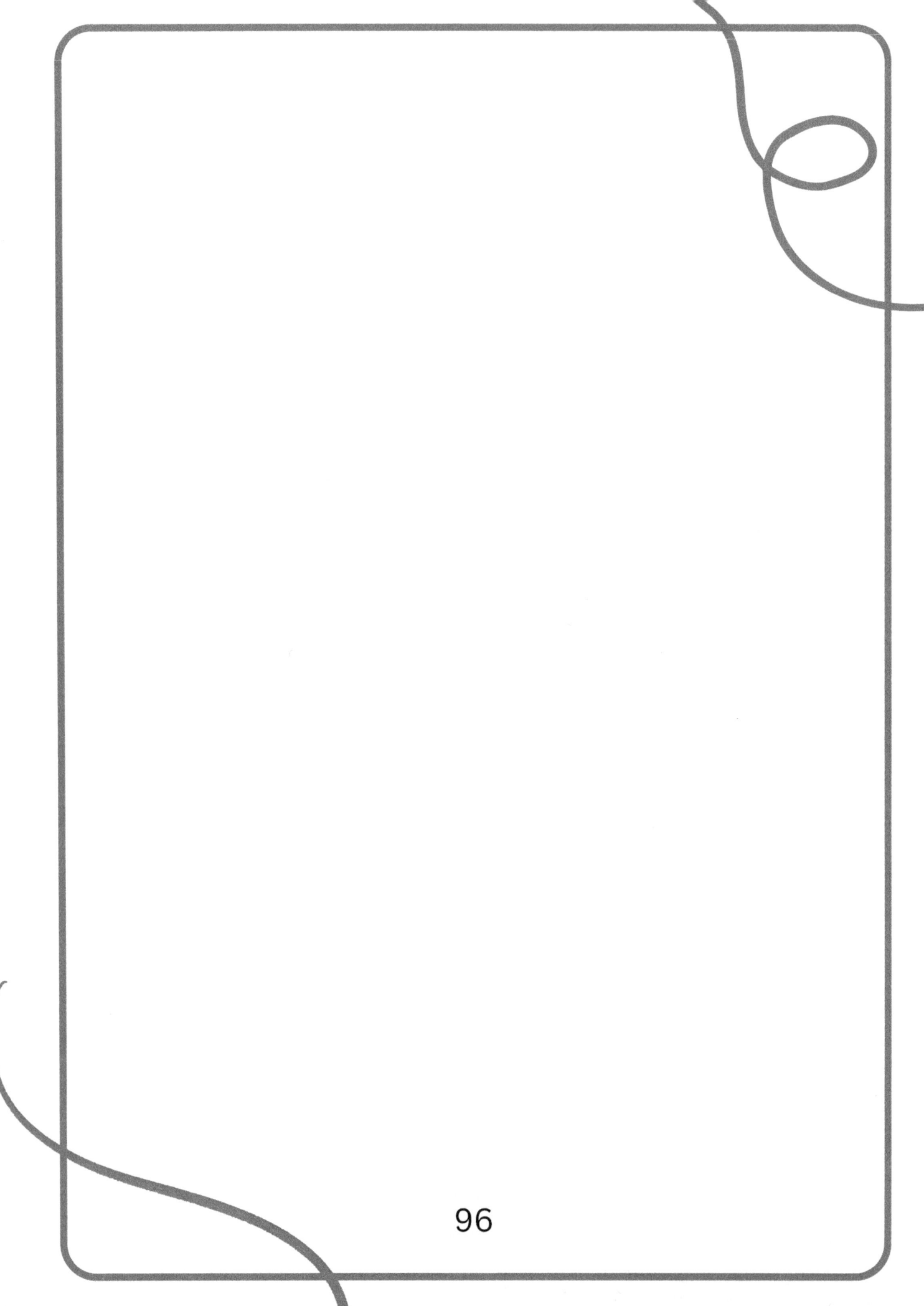